Second Edition

COACHING TO CHANGE LIVES

Dennis Parker
D.W. Rutledge

ISBN: 1-58518-993-6
Library of Congress Control Number: 2006931484
Cover design: Studio J Art & Design
Book layout: Studio J Art & Design
Front cover photo: Scott Halleran/Getty Images Sport

Coaches Choice
P.O. Box 1828
Monterey, CA 93942
www.coacheschoice.com

Dedication

To all those who have chosen the coaching profession, may your influence be positive, your leadership be true, and your example be strong.

Acknowledgments

There are many people who have made this curriculum possible. I have never considered myself an author, but rather someone who gleaned a lot of stories, quotes, and facts from some really great people. Wilson Mizner said, "When you take stuff from one writer, it's plagiarism; but when you take it from many writers, it's research." So by that definition, I consider myself a Ph.D. in research.

First, I want to thank my parents. I will always be amazed at how they could instill in six boys a core value system and an enormous pride in being a Parker—without any material possessions. I often wish I could have been half as good a parent to my two kids as Sam and Bert Parker were to me.

I would also like to thank Bob Wilmoth in Idabel, Oklahoma who taught me how to coach "kids," and Val Reneau at Southeastern Oklahoma University who taught me how to coach football.

In addition, I want to acknowledge my "partners" Rose Nunn (Cleburne, TX), Jayne Fletcher (Keller, TX), and Patsy Gardner (Odessa, TX), for the work and time that they put into making this curriculum possible and for their help in promoting and supporting me while we were together.

Finally, I'd like to thank my beautiful wife, Merry Metcalf, for ALWAYS being there. Without her, I could never be the Dennis Parker that I am. She is definitely the "wind beneath my wings."

—D.P.

The first and most important team in anyone's life is their family. In my life, that means Kathy, thirty-five years my wife and my wife forevermore. We have been partners in life and in developing our philosophies and beliefs; also, my son, Clint, who has been a true inspiration to me in all phases of his life. He played for me and coached for me and has grown into a man of whom I am extremely proud. They have both been a strong influence in my life.

I would also like to thank the coaches and players with whom I have had the privilege to work over the years. Each of these individuals in their own way have taught me much about competition, discipline, and caring. They have all blessed my life in so many ways.

—D.W.R.

Contents

Mental training—how important is it in the development of your athletes? All of us have heard from the great coaches that the game is 90 percent mental and only 10 percent physical, yet it seems that we spend all of our time on the physical development of our athletes.

We are discovering that we have been overeducated on the physical aspects of sports training and undereducated on the mental aspects. We have a new awareness of the power of the mind, the power of thought. It is the driving force of our existence. What we think and what we concentrate on is what we become.

We have always been impressed by the philosophy that a man becomes what he thinks; that a man's character is the outward expression of his inner thoughts. But it is not a new philosophy. It is an ancient philosophy that you can trace all the way back to the sacred literature of the Hindus: "Man becomes that which he thinks." You can find it eloquently expressed in the writings of Buddha: "The mind is everything—what you think you become…" You can find it in the meditations of Marcus Aurelius: "Your life is what your thoughts make it." You can find the same basic idea in the writings of Confucius, Mohammed, Aristotle, Socrates, and scores of others. It is also found in the Bible: "As a man thinketh in his heart, so is he" (Proverbs 23:7).

In 1902, an educator and writer named James Allen wrote a book titled, *As a Man Thinketh*, in which he makes a very powerful statement that can help your athletes understand a very important principle of success in life. "The divinity that shapes our end is in ourselves…All that a man achieves or fails to achieve is the direct result of his own thoughts."

Mental training can have a powerful impact on our programs and, more importantly, a life-changing impact on our athletes. Participation in a positive athletic program with coaches who are good role models can be a life-changing experience for many kids.

Our young people are in need of strong role models more today than at any other time in our history. Many parents are divorced; a strong father figure is absent in many homes. What we find in many juvenile courts is that 80 percent of the court dockets are filled with youngsters who come from divided homes. On top of that, we have the most powerful media communication in the history of mankind, barraging us every day with negative messages regarding violence, drugs and alcohol, pornography, terrorism, and anything that might sell newspapers and air time.

A void exists within many of our young people that needs to be filled. It is important that the void be filled with positive thoughts and not negative thoughts. As coaches, we can be a part of the problem or a part of the solution. We believe that our athletic programs and our coaches can have a tremendous impact on our schools and communities and a life-changing impact on our young people. The *Coaching to Change Lives* curriculum can give you a plan to do just that.

Athletics can be more than just playing a game. It is possible to use an athletic program as a vehicle to develop the total person. No doubt exists that young people can grow morally, intellectually, physically, and spiritually through a properly directed athletic program.

Coaching can and should be one of the most influential professions in our entire society. As coaches, we have been given an incredible platform from which to deal with hundreds of young people on almost a daily basis.

Young people today, more than at any other time in the history of education, are desperate for love, discipline, and direction. What we are doing to develop the hearts and minds of our young people is much more important than any physical training we can give them or any skills we can teach them.

Through this *Coaching to Change Lives* curriculum, we will show you how we have implemented, over the past 16 years, the ideas and methods that we have acquired from Zig Ziglar's "I CAN" course and many other programs and individuals. The curriculum consists of things that have worked well for us and that we have a strong belief in.

Good, old-fashioned values are the most important factors an athletic program has to offer the educational process. Such values include self-discipline, responsibility, accountability, leadership, loyalty, and more. If young people are to face the challenges of today's world, they will need those time-tested values more than ever before.

Good luck in your endeavors to develop a better person as well as a better athlete.

—Dennis Parker
—D.W. Rutledge

Congratulations! The principles of the course you are about to teach have changed hundreds of thousands of lives *for the better*. Both the team and each individual student benefit from participation in this easy-to-implement program. We want to give you an understanding of the course format to help make this a successful learning experience for you and your students.

Format Explanation

Each lesson includes a worksheet that you should copy for each student, as well as all the necessary instructions you need to teach the class. The components for each lesson are as follows:

Say: This information is provided in a narrative format for you to adapt to your own style of teaching; it is not a script to be read verbatim. Rather, it is a suggestion of how to introduce a lesson. Timing guidelines are presented for each "Say" section.

Do: Step-by-step procedures are given for each worksheet. Again, timing guidelines are given.

Worksheet: The activities in each lesson have been carefully selected to provide elements of self-discovery and opportunities to practice building skills in the relatively safe environment of the classroom.

For discussion: These questions are designed to let the students think for themselves and hear other students' views. It is important that you allow the students to do most of the talking during this section.

Word of the day: Every lesson includes a particular word to be learned and its corresponding definition. After reviewing the word, have a student use the word in a sentence.

"If you take a man as he is, you make him worse than he was, but if you see him as being the best person possible, then he, in fact, becomes the best person possible."
—Anonymous

See the good in your players and inspire them to use the talents they have. Coach up!

1. Super good!
2. You've got it made.
3. Super!
4. That's right!
5. That's good.
6. You're really working hard today.
7. You are very good at that.
8. That's coming along nicely.
9. Good work!
10. That's better!
11. I'm happy to see you working like that.
12. Exactly right.
13. I'm proud of the way you worked today.
14. You are doing that much better today.
15. You've just about got it.
16. That's the best you have ever done.
17. You're doing a good job.
18. That's it!
19. Now you've figured it out.
20. That's quite an improvement.
21. Great!
22. I knew you could do it.
23. Congratulations!
24. Not bad.
25. Keep working on it, you're improving.
26. Now you have it!
27. You are learning fast.
28. Good for you!
29. Couldn't have done it better myself.
30. You are a joy.
31. One more time and you'll have it.
32. You really make my job fun.
33. That's the right way to do it.
34. You're getting better every day.
35. You did it that time!
36. You're on the right track now.
37. Nice going.
38. You haven't missed a thing.
39. Wow!
40. That's the way!
41. Keep up the good work.
42. Terrific!
43. Nothing can stop you now.
44. That's the way to do it.
45. Sensational!
46. You've got your brain in gear today.
47. That's better.
48. That was first-class work.
49. Excellent!
50. That's the best ever.
51. You've just about mastered that.
52. Perfect!
53. That's better than ever.
54. Much better!
55. Wonderful!
56. You must have been practicing!
57. You did that very well.
58. Fine!
59. Nice job.
60. You're really going to town.
61. Outstanding!
62. Fantastic!
63. Tremendous!
64. That's how to handle that!
65. Now that's what I call a fine job.
66. That's great.
67. Right on!
68. You're really improving.

69. You're doing beautifully.
70. Superb!
71. Good remembering!
72. You've got that down pat.
73. You certainly did well today.
74. Keep it up!
75. Congratulations. You got it right.
76. You did a lot of work today.
77. Well, look at you go!
78. That's perfect!
79. I'm very proud of you.
80. Marvelous!
81. I like that.
82. Way to go!
83. Now you have the hang of it!
84. You're doing fine.
85. Good thinking.
86. You are really learning a lot!
87. Good going.
88. I've never seen anyone do it better.
89. Keep on trying!
90. You outdid yourself today!
91. Good for you!
92. I think you've got it now.
93. That's a good (boy/girl).
94. Good job, [student's name].
95. You figured that out fast.
96. You remembered!
97. That's really nice.
98. That kind of work makes me happy.
99. It's such a pleasure to teach when you work like that!

DEVELOPING
A BASE

Photo Credit: Ronald Martinez/Getty Images Sport

"He who stops being better, stops being good."

—Oliver Cromwell

Chapter 1

DEVELOPING VOCABULARY—COACH'S NOTES

SAY: (5 MINUTES)

It has been proven that you can increase your IQ by improving your vocabulary. This part of the curriculum was added several years ago because of concern over the fact that a number of otherwise intelligent students were not passing their college entrance exams. Tests indicated that the students' vocabularies were woefully inadequate. In an attempt to rectify the situation, a few teachers then began introducing the students to a new vocabulary word each day, causing their scores to improve.

Even if you're not interested in taking college entrance exams, these vocabulary words will give you a better command of the English language. The key point that should be emphasized is that your vocabulary should never limit you from reaching your potential.

Each week you will have the opportunity to learn new vocabulary words. These words are connected to the lessons, and were chosen to help you develop your language skills. Each day you will be given a vocabulary word and its definition. Start using these words in your daily conversation. The words will be reviewed once each week.

DO: (15 MINUTES)

- Lead a discussion from the questions on the student worksheet. Be sure to let the students do the talking and always ask for specific examples.
- Review the word of the day. Ask a student to use it correctly in a sentence.

DEVELOPING VOCABULARY—WORKSHEET

"Genius without education is like silver in the mine."

—Benjamin Franklin

For discussion:

1. Imagine yourself in a room full of people where no one speaks your language. How would you feel?

_____

_____

_____

_____

_____

_____

2. Increasing your vocabulary will help you reach your potential. Explain.

_____

_____

_____

_____

_____

_____

_____

Word of the Day: Intelligence—the ability to learn or understand or to deal with new or trying situations

DEVELOPING GRATITUDE—COACH'S NOTES

SAY: (5 MINUTES)

Gratitude is defined as being appreciative of what you have. Every day you will be asked to write three statements of gratitude. If you consistently recognize everything that you have, you will be a happier person. However, gratitude is not durable and must be reinforced daily. Grateful people may be thought of as those who always see the glass as half full while ungrateful people see the same glass as half empty.

- If you have money in the bank, in your wallet, and spare change in a dish someplace, you are among the top 8 percent of the world's wealthiest people.
- If you woke up this morning with more health than illness, you are more blessed than the million people who won't survive this week.
- If you have never experienced the danger of battle, the loneliness of imprisonment, the agony of torture, or the pangs of starvation, you are ahead of 20 million people around the world.
- If you have food in the refrigerator, clothes on your back, a roof over your head, and a place to sleep, you are richer than 75 percent of this world.
- If you attend a church meeting without the fear of harassment, arrest, torture, or death, you are more blessed than almost three billion people in this world.
- If you can read this message, you are more blessed than more than two billion people in the world who cannot read anything at all.
- If you hold up your head with a smile on your face and are truly thankful, you are blessed, because the majority of people can, but most do not.

Sometimes you may take for granted the most important things and people in your life. Every one of you has influences that create a special impact and make you who you are. You will take time each day to write down what you are grateful for. Gratitude will make you a happier, more productive person.

DO: (15 MINUTES)

- Lead a discussion from the questions on the student worksheet. Be sure to let the students do the talking and always ask for specific examples.
- Review the word of the day. Ask a student to use it correctly in a sentence.

DEVELOPING GRATITUDE—WORKSHEET

"Gratitude makes sense of our past, brings peace for today, and creates vision for tomorrow."

—John F. Kennedy

1. What are the characteristics of an ungrateful person?

_____

_____

_____

_____

_____

2. Why is it important to be grateful?

_____

_____

_____

_____

_____

3. Why doesn't gratitude last?

_____

_____

_____

_____

_____

Word of the Day: Gratitude—the state of being appreciative of the benefits you have received; thankfulness

DEVELOPING DIRECTION—COACH'S NOTES

SAY: (5 MINUTES)

Imagine attempting to play a game of basketball with no goals (rims and backboards). You would never know if you scored or missed, if you were short or long. Yet 97 percent of Americans go to work each day without goals. They may not be playing the game of basketball, but they are playing the game of life without goals. They do not know how well or how poorly they are doing, which makes it impossible for them to focus on the results of their actions.

Daily objectives help you become results-oriented instead of time-oriented. What you accomplish is determined by your objectives. Fifty percent of getting something done is first putting it in writing.

Daily objectives may be done as a group or as individual. A student's daily objectives may focus on academics, extracurricular activities, or home life. Individual objectives may relate to a task to be done that day. Or an objective may be directed toward accomplishing a larger goal. A class or group may set daily objectives as part of a group goal for the week.

Friedrich Nietzsche, a renowned 19th century German philosopher said, "If you have a why to live for, the how doesn't matter." The "why" is a worthwhile goal you wish to accomplish—pass chemistry, win a championship, or land the job you've always wanted. Your daily objectives are the "how" in accomplishing the "why." Large goals— the "why"—need short-term intermediate steps. Large goals are not accomplished by one grand effort or action, but rather by consistent smaller actions that move you closer to the goal on a daily basis. Daily objectives will help you maintain direction and progress toward the achievements you truly desire from life.

DO: (15 MINUTES)

- Lead a discussion from the questions on the student worksheet. Be sure to let the students do the talking and always ask for specific examples.
- Review the word of the day. Ask a student to use it correctly in a sentence.

DEVELOPING DIRECTION—WORKSHEET

"Without some goal and some effort to reach it, no one can live."
—Fyodor Dostoevsky

1. Share an example of a time you have been time-oriented, rather than results-oriented.

   _____

   _____

   _____

   _____

   _____

2. Why is it important to have a "why?"

   _____

   _____

   _____

   _____

   _____

3. What is your "why" for this class?

   _____

   _____

   _____

   _____

   _____

Word of the Day: Direction—a guiding, governing, or motivating purpose; a channel or direct course of thought or action

DEVELOPING A BETTER "YOU"—COACH'S NOTES

SAY: (5 MINUTES)

Each lesson is designed to help you develop your character. The lessons are made up of stories, poems, commentaries, and personal experiences that will hopefully "pull out" something that you might have overlooked. Each day, you will hear a lesson and have a short discussion. You will sometimes be divided into small groups to focus on a specific aspect of what you just learned. The entire group will then discuss the lesson as a whole and go over your answers to the questions. To develop character, everyone's input is necessary.

The following story illustrates an important point. On the first day of a graduate class, the professor came in, and without a word, began handing out 3" x 5" cards containing clues to a murder mystery. Each of the nine students in the class received six cards. The teacher then explained that the group would be dismissed when the clues on the cards were used to solve the who, what, where, why, and how of the mystery. After an hour or so, the group asked if they could take a break. The professor told them to keep working.

The graduate class was a three-hour evening class from 6:00–9:00 pm. At about 8:30, the professor asked if the group had solved the mystery. When they could not answer any of the questions, he said that someone had a "ringer" card. The person who had the ringer card, the one who had not taken part in any aspect of the group discussion, then read from a card, "Do not give out any information unless it is expressly and persistently asked." When he did share his clues, the mystery was easily solved.

The professor's point was made. During that semester, the graduate class made sure to include every person in the discussion. You never know who might have the answer.

DO: (15 MINUTES)

- Lead a discussion from the questions on the student worksheet. Be sure to let the students do the talking and always ask for specific examples.
- Review the word of the day. Ask a student to use it correctly in a sentence.

TEACHING THE LESSONS—WORKSHEET

"Nothing in life is to be feared. It is only to be understood."

—Marie Curie

1. Why is it important to share your thoughts and ideas?

   _____

   _____

   _____

   _____

   _____

2. Why is this sometimes difficult to do?

   _____

   _____

   _____

   _____

   _____

3. Is there anything you can do to make it easier for a classmate to share his or her ideas with the class?

   _____

   _____

   _____

   _____

   _____

Word of the Day: Persist—to go on resolutely or stubbornly in spite of opposition, importunity, or warning

ATTITUDE

Photo Credit: Elsa/Getty Images Sport

Chapter 2

"Nothing can stop the man with the right mental attitude from achieving his goal; nothing on earth can help the man with the wrong mental attitude."

—W.W. Ziege

IMPORTANCE OF A PROPER MENTAL ATTITUDE—COACH'S NOTES

SAY: (5 MINUTES)

A proper attitude is undoubtedly the key to success. The most important thing that a teacher can do is help his students understand the importance of having a proper mental attitude.

Consider the following statements regarding mental attitude:

- More than 50,000 schools exist in America that will teach students how to do everything from trimming toenails and fingernails to how to operate heavy machinery to how to become a doctor or a lawyer. However, no school can teach someone how to be any better than mediocre unless that person has the proper mental attitude.

- Your attitude as you undertake a project is the most dominant factor in the success of that project. In short, your attitude is really more important than your aptitude.

- Charles Swindoll said the following about attitude: "The longer I live, the more I realize the impact of attitude on life. Attitude, to me, is more important than facts. It is more important than the past, than education, than money, than circumstances, than failures, than successes, than what other people think or say or do. It is more important than appearance, giftedness, or skill. It will make or break a company…a church…a home. The remarkable thing is we have a choice every day regarding the attitude we embrace for that day. We cannot change our past…we cannot change the fact that people will act in a certain way. We cannot change the inevitable. The only thing we can do is play on the one string we have, and that is our attitude…I am convinced that life is 10 percent what happens to me and 90 percent how I react to it. And so it is with you…we are in charge of our attitudes."

If attitude is that important—then what exactly is it? If you look attitude up in the dictionary, it says, "A manner of thinking, acting, or feeling." Your attitude, then, is how you think. What you do always comes after what you think. What you allow to influence your mind determines what you think. What you think, in turn, determines the choices you make. The choices you make then determine the habits you develop. The habits you develop determine who you are and what you will become, because when you choose a habit you choose the end result of that habit.

Consider the following examples of attitudes that each person chooses every day. These choices either move you toward your goals or keep you from reaching them.

- Enthusiasm versus a sour disposition
- Hard work versus laziness
- Persistent effort versus quitting
- Commitment versus going along with the crowd
- Love versus hate

The little yes's and no's that you choose each day will determine who you are, what you have, and what you will become 10 years from now. The difference between accomplishment and failure is simply having a proper mental attitude.

DO: (15 MINUTES)

- Discuss Question #1 on the student worksheet.
- Have the students work in pairs or small groups to answer Question #2 on the student worksheet and then have the groups report their answers back to the class.
- Review the word of the day. Ask a student to use it correctly in a sentence.

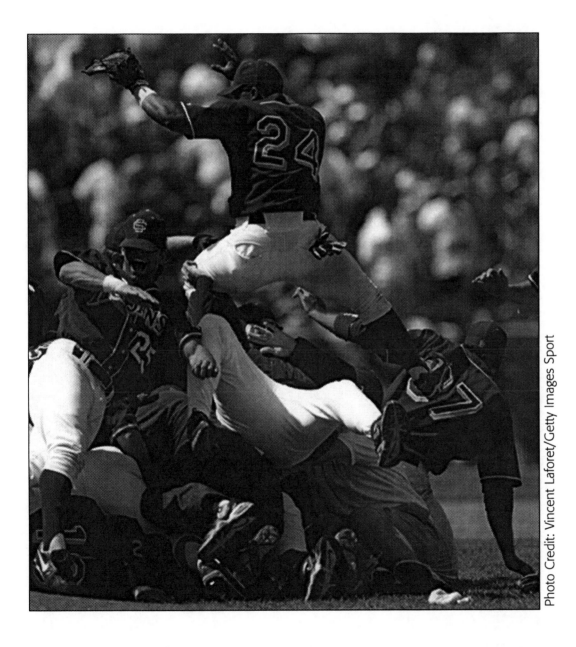

Photo Credit: Vincent Laforet/Getty Images Sport

IMPORTANCE OF A PROPER MENTAL ATTITUDE— WORKSHEET

"Do not attempt to do a thing unless you are sure of yourself; but do not relinquish it simply because someone else is not sure of you."

—Stewart E. White

For discussion:

1. What is attitude?

    _____

    _____

    _____

    _____

    _____

    _____

2. Give three examples of positive attitudes and three examples of negative attitudes that affect your life on a daily basis.

    Positive:

    •

    •

    •

    Negative:

    •

    •

    •

Word of the Day: Achievement—gain by work or effort; a great or heroic deed.

AS A MAN THINKETH, SO IS HE—COACH'S NOTES

LESSON #2

SAY: (5 MINUTES)

Ancient philosophy states that a man becomes that which he thinks and that a man's character is the outward expression of his inward thoughts. That philosophy can be traced all the way back to the *Meditations* of Marcus Aurelius, in which he wrote: "Your life is what your thoughts make it."

The same basic idea is found in the writings of Aristotle, Socrates, and scores of others. It is found in its most familiar form in the Bible (Proverbs 23:7): "As he thinketh in his heart, so is he."

James Allen, an educator, wrote *As a Man Thinketh* in 1905. In his book, he makes a very powerful statement—a statement that every coach should have solidly in his mind. It is a statement that can help your athletes understand a very important principle of success in life: "The divinity that shapes our ends is in ourselves…all that a man achieves or fails to achieve is the direct result of his own thoughts."

In this statement, Allen teaches two essential truths:
- Today, you are where your thoughts have taken you.
- You are the architect—for better or worse—of your future.

It seems as if people are forever complaining about things outside themselves, blaming their condition and circumstances on everything but their own thoughts and ideas. It is important that people realize that they make their own "good fortune," that their lives are the result of their own thinking. Strong thoughts generate strong actions, while weak thoughts generate weak actions. A man is literally what he thinks. Who you are and what you become are a direct result of your own thoughts. A man can only rise, conquer, and achieve by lifting up his thoughts.

DO: (15 MINUTES)

- Lead a discussion from the questions on the student worksheet. Be sure to let the students do the talking and always ask for specific examples.
- Review the word of the day. Ask a student to use it correctly in a sentence.

AS A MAN THINKETH, SO IS HE—WORKSHEET

"To see what is right, and not do it, is want of courage or of principle."

—Confucius

For discussion:

1. What does the following statement mean? "The divinity that shapes our ends is in ourselves…all that a man achieves or fails to achieve is the direct result of his own thoughts."

    _____

    _____

    _____

    _____

2. Do you agree? Why or why not?

    _____

    _____

    _____

    _____

3. List some examples in which positive or negative thoughts have impacted your life.

    _____

    _____

    _____

    _____

Word of the Day: Perception—physical sensation interpreted in the light of experience; mental image

YOUR GREATEST POWER—COACH'S NOTES

SAY: (5 MINUTES)

Ralph Waldo Emerson once said, "Great leaders are those who understand that thoughts rule the world." The greatest power you have is the power to choose what thoughts will dominate your mind. How you think will determine what you become. The following statement should dominate your thinking: "I am a winner in life."

The following story illustrates how winners think: Bernardo Castro was an immigrant to the United States. He came to New York City with only a couple of dollars. He searched from store to store to find a job. Finally, he got a job sweeping out an upholstery shop. He could not speak English, so he enrolled in night school. It was a large school of more than 2,000 students. One cold December night he set out to go to class. He had to walk five miles and a blizzard was raging. After going one block, the thought came to him, "Turn around and go back." The other thought he had was, "I can make it. Keep going." He decided to keep on going. At each block, as the cold and misery grew worse, he decided to keep going. When he reached the school the door was locked. Finally, a janitor came to the door and told him that no one had shown up because of the weather and that the school was closed. Bernardo turned and began his long walk home. He was frustrated and miserable, but after traveling about a mile, he began to feel happy and excited. He walked taller and straighter, with pride in every step, as he thought, "Of more than 2,000 people, I am the only one who had the guts to weather the storm. I've got something great inside of me. My destiny is to achieve greatness."

Bernardo Castro would gradually go from sweeping up an upholstery shop to being an apprentice to an upholsterer, to being an upholsterer, to being a furniture-store salesman. Then, he managed a furniture store, became a furniture-store owner, and eventually the owner of a chain of furniture stores and a millionaire. The key to his success was that he saw himself as a winner.

The key point that is reflected in Bernard Castro's actions is the power of positive thinking. You must always think in terms of investing for greater returns. Work, effort, time, practice, and sacrifice are all simply forms of investment. The more you invest, the greater will be the return. You must always remember that life is what you make it. If you want to win, you must work like a winner. All the work, effort, and pain you invest will someday be remembered in terms of great pride. However, only a few receive the great returns, because only a few are willing to make the great investments.

A man who thinks of himself as a winner must realize that winners get after it and make it happen. Losers are quick to see why things can't be done, while winners set about the business of doing things. Winners work. Losers gripe. Winners fight. Losers quit. Winners smile and laugh and enjoy life. Losers become cynical, depressed, suspicious of others, and find little joy in life.

Ask yourself, "What do I want to be in life, a winner or a loser?" You can choose either one. It depends on how you think. It depends on how you work. It depends on you.

DO: (15 MINUTES)

- Lead the group in a discussion of the questions found on the student worksheet.
- You may want to add a sense of competition to Question #3. Divide the group into smaller teams and give them four minutes to brainstorm as many answers as they can. Give the group with the most ideas a small prize.
- Review the word of the day. Ask a student to use it correctly in a sentence.

Photo Credit: Brian Bahr/Getty Images Sport

YOUR GREATEST POWER—WORKSHEET

"It is hard to fail, but it is worse never to have tried to succeed. In this life we get nothing save by effort."

—Theodore Roosevelt

For discussion:

1. What does the following statement mean? "Work, effort, time, practice, and sacrifice are all simply forms of investments. The more you invest, the greater will be the return."

   _____

   _____

   _____

   _____

2. Do you agree? Why or why not?

   _____

   _____

   _____

   _____

3. List some specific things that you can be investing in for great returns in life.

   _____

   _____

   _____

   _____

Word of the Day: Effort—use of resources toward a goal

LESSON #4

ANSWER THE CALL—COACH'S NOTES

SAY: (5 MINUTES)

All of life is a series of choices and what you choose to give life today will determine what life will give you tomorrow. You must accept total responsibility for those choices. How you think, how you react, and the choices you make are totally up to you. Those choices are going to determine who you are, what you have, and what you are going to become 10 years down the road. Some of those choices are easy, but some of them are very tough. It is those tough choices that separate the men from the boys and identify the truly strong and committed individuals.

Consider the following story about tough choices and commitment: Legend has it that centuries ago Mohammed set out to develop the finest strain of horses in the world. He sent out his 50 best men to search the world for the 100 finest horses. In six months, they returned with the very finest horses in the world. Mohammed trained them himself. It took him six months. He trained the horses to respond to his command every time he blew his silver trumpet.

When he was convinced that they were fully trained, that he could do no more, he took them to the desert to a place where it never got below 120 degrees. He corralled them on a small hill overlooking an oasis of bubbling cool water 100 yards away and gave them nothing to eat or drink. At the end of three days, they were at each others' throats. They were frantic! They could be contained no longer.

Then came the supreme test. Mohammed ordered his men to open the corral gates. Now can't you just see those 100 horses stampeding toward the oasis of water? When they got within 100 feet of the water—then came the test. Mohammed blew that trumpet one more time. Lo and behold—one horse yielded, reluctantly, obediently, to the master and came. From that one horse was raised the Arabian strain, the finest strain of horses in the world today. The message is this—that one out of 100 answers the really tough calls and makes the really tough choices. One out of 100 is truly committed.

Those people who want to be the very best that they can be must be willing to answer the tough calls. They must be willing to make the tough choices.

One of the toughest choices you have to make is overcoming "peer pressure." You have to be willing to say "no" to those things that can keep you from your goals and dreams. Even when it seems as if the rest of the world is saying "yes," you must have the strength of character to stick to those things that you know to be right, and to refuse those things that you know to be wrong.

DO: (15 MINUTES)

- Lead the group in a discussion of the questions found on the student worksheet.
- Review the word of the day. Ask a student to use it correctly in a sentence.

ANSWER THE CALL—WORKSHEET

"He who has learned to obey will know how to command."

—Solon

For discussion:

1. Give at least three examples of tough choices young people today have to make in overcoming peer pressure.

_____

_____

_____

_____

_____

_____

_____

2. Give some examples of situations in athletics where answering "tough calls" makes you a better athlete.

_____

_____

_____

_____

_____

_____

_____

_____

Word of the Day: Discipline—control gained by obedience or training

DETERMINATION: DECIDING TO HANG TOUGH—COACH'S NOTES

SAY: (5 MINUTES)

Success depends on "staying power," or the ability to "hang tough" regardless of the situation. Trying once just doesn't get the job done; you've got to try and try again. A lack of determination and persistence is the reason most people fail in attaining their goals.

The following quote by Calvin Coolidge provides some great words to live by and points out the importance of persistence: *Press on. Nothing in the world can take the place of persistence. Talent will not; nothing is more common than unsuccessful individuals with talent. Genius will not; unrewarded genius is almost a proverb. Education will not; the world is full of educated derelicts. Persistence and determination alone are omnipotent.*

It seems that coaches are always coming into contact with people who have been misled, thinking that success depends solely on talent or brilliance or education. Or they believe that success depends upon getting the breaks, knowing the right people, or being in the right place at the right time.

In fact, the thing that makes for greatness is determination—persisting in the right direction over the long haul, following your dream, staying at the task. Just as instant failure does not exist, neither does automatic or instant success. But success is the direct result of a process that is long, difficult, and often unappreciated by others. It also includes a willingness to sacrifice and a relentless effort to hang tough in the tough situations. Persistence and determination in action can be defined as follows: "When you keep working while others choose to quit."

Consider this story about a man who loved to hunt: The man bought two pups that were top-notch bird dogs. He kept them in his backyard, where he trained them. One morning, an ornery little vicious-looking bulldog came shuffling and snorting down the alley. He crawled under the fence into the backyard with the bird dogs. It was easy to see that he meant business. The man's first impulse was to take his setters and lock them in the basement so they wouldn't tear up that little bulldog; but he decided he would let the little bulldog learn a lesson he would never forget.

Naturally, the dogs got into a scuffle in the backyard and those two bird dogs and that bulldog went round and round. Growls and yips were heard as bulldog hair flew everywhere. The little critter finally had enough, so he squeezed under the fence and took off. All the rest of the day he whined and licked his sores. Interestingly, the next day at about the same time that same ornery little bulldog crawled back under the fence and after those bird dogs. Once again, the bird dogs beat the stuffing out of that little animal and would have chewed him up if he hadn't retreated down the alley. Would you believe that the very next day he was back? Same time, same situation, same results. Once again, after the bulldog had all he could take, he crawled back under the fence and found his way home to lick his wounds.

The man had to leave town on business and was gone for several weeks. When he came back, he asked his wife what had happened. She told him that every day at the same time that little bulldog came back and fought with his two bird dogs. He never missed a day. It was to the point that when those bird dogs heard the bulldog snorting down the alley and spotted him squeezing under the fence they immediately started whining and ran down into the basement. That little bulldog strutted around the backyard like he owned it. That bulldog had "staying power."

The story of the bulldog is an example of persistence and determination—staying at it, hanging tough with dogged discipline. When you get whipped or when you win, the secret is staying at it.

DO: (15 MINUTES)

- Lead a large group discussion of Question #1. Make sure that everyone has a good understanding of the two terms.
- For Questions #2 and #3, allow a few minutes for each student to answer. Then divide the large group into smaller groups of four people. Allow each person to share his examples. At the end of the discussion, you may want to ask for one or two examples to be shared with the large group.
- Review the word of the day. Ask a student to use it correctly in a sentence.

Photo Credit: Doug Pensinger/Getty Images Sport

DETERMINATION: DECIDING TO HANG TOUGH— WORKSHEET

"There is no failure except in no longer trying. There is no defeat except from within, no really insurmountable barrier save our own inherent weakness of purpose."

—Kin Hubbard

For discussion:

1. How do you define persistence and determination?

_____

_____

_____

_____

_____

2. Give an example of an experience in your life or someone you know in which success resulted from persistence.

_____

_____

_____

_____

3. Give an example of an experience in your life or someone you know in which failure to reach a goal resulted from a lack of persistence.

_____

_____

_____

_____

Word of the Day: Perseverance—to persist in a state of opposition or discouragement

PRACTICE ATTITUDE—COACH'S NOTES

SAY: (5 MINUTES)

It is important for you to understand that you will perform during the season exactly as you practice. The following statement regarding "practice attitude" includes some thoughts that you should carry with you to practice each day.

Practice does not make perfect—practice makes permanent. No matter what you do, if you practice long enough it will become a part of you. Practice a bad habit and you will become great at a bad habit. Practice being second class and you will be second class. Practice being first class and you will be first class. The choices you make in tough situations will be the habits you develop. Remember, when you choose a habit, you also choose the end result of that habit.

The habits you choose in the off-season, in summer training, and in your daily workouts will be what you become as a team. The habits you choose in practice will be the habits you will revert to when it gets tough in the fourth quarter of a tight ball game. You will perform during the season exactly as you practice.

Your practice attitude is the key to your success as a team. Remember the following quote: "What you do speaks so loudly, I can't hear what you say." Albert Einstein once said, "Example is not the best way to teach, it is the only way." Leaders are leaders because of what they do, not what they say they are going to do. Every player must strive to be an example, demonstrating class, discipline, aggressiveness, and total effort.

When you practice, work to accomplish something—work to get better. Many people confuse activity with accomplishment. Putting in time or attending workouts ensures nothing. It does not matter where you start. What matters is where you finish. Every practice, every workout, is an opportunity for you to get better individually and as a team. The way you practice as a team will be the way you will play as a team.

DO: (15 MINUTES)

- Lead the group in a discussion of the questions on the student worksheet. Remember to let the students do most of the talking during this time.
- Spend the majority of the discussion time on the last question.
- Review the word of the day. Ask a student to use it correctly in a sentence.

PRACTICE ATTITUDE—WORKSHEET

"Diligence is the mother of good luck."

—Benjamin Franklin

For discussion:

1. What does the following statement mean? "Practice does not make perfect—practice makes permanent."

    _____

    _____

    _____

2. Do you agree? Why or why not?

    _____

    _____

    _____

3. "What you do speaks so loudly, I can't hear what you say." What does this statement mean to you?

    _____

    _____

    _____

4. What can you do as a team to make your "practice attitude" better?

    _____

    _____

    _____

Word of the Day: Diligence—steady, earnest, and energetic effort

ENTHUSIASM: A WINNING SPIRIT!—COACH'S NOTES

SPECIAL NOTE

An athletic program must always be planned so that it spreads and develops enthusiasm. Like everything else, it starts with the coach. You must love life, love the game, and love your players. You must encourage and excite your players to become their best. Your enthusiasm must be contagious. You must create the environment and provide the motivation so that it becomes a habit to play the game enthusiastically.

SAY: (5 MINUTES)

Harry Truman, the 33rd President, said, "The successful man has enthusiasm. Good work is never done in cold blood; heat and fire are needed to forge anything solid. Every great achievement is the story of a flaming heart."

Enthusiasm is adding emotion to your efforts. A player without enthusiasm is like a fire without wind. The fire will burn, but it will never be a raging blaze. The player will try, but only enough to "just get by." When he becomes enthusiastic, however, he becomes an uncontrollable flame of intense effort. He becomes emotional.

The unenthusiastic player is like a man carrying an anvil on his back. He drags around, barely able to move. He's bored with everything and many times feels sorry for himself. It is important you realize how lucky you are and how many blessings and talents you have. You need to see the benefits that can come from using your talents as opposed to wasting them. Your potential is infinite and extends beyond your wildest imagination. You have been given everything you need. Your only limitations are those you place on yourself.

The following poem points out the unique power of enthusiasm.

Enthusiasm

Enthusiasm! That certain something that makes us great—that pulls us out of the mediocre and commonplace—that builds into us power. It glows and shines, it lights up our faces. Enthusiasm, the keynote that makes us sing and makes men sing with us.

Enthusiasm—the maker of friends—the maker of smiles—the producer of confidence. It cries to the world, "I've got what it takes." It tells all men that your job is a great job—the company you work for just suits you—the goods you have are the best.

Enthusiasm—the inspiration that makes you "wake up and live." It puts spring in your step—spring in your heart—a twinkle in your eyes—confidence in yourself and your fellow man.
Enthusiasm is reason gone mad to achieve a definite, rational objective.

Enthusiasm is inflamed by opposition, but never converted; it's the leaping lightning that blasts obstacles from its path.

Enthusiasm is a contagion that laughs at quarantine and inoculates all who come in contact with it.

Enthusiasm is the vibrant thrill in your voice that sways the wills of others into harmony with your own.

Enthusiasm is the "philosopher's stone" that transmutes dull tasks into delightful deeds.

Enthusiasm is a magnet that draws kindred souls with irresistible force and electrifies them with magnetism of its own resolves.

Enthusiasm—do you have it? Then thank God for it. If you haven't got it— then get down on your knees and pray for it.

DO: (15 MINUTES)

- Lead the group in the discussion of the questions on the student worksheet. Be sure to stress that attitude (enthusiasm) is a choice that players can make. You don't always feel enthusiastic, but you can choose to behave that way and the emotion of enthusiasm will come.
- Divide the group into smaller work teams for Question #3. Allow them three or four minutes to devise a way to get the rest of the group excited. Have each group actually show their idea in class, or use the different groups during the next several practice sessions when enthusiasm begins to lag.
- Review the word of the day. Ask a student to use it correctly in a sentence.

ENTHUSIASM: A WINNING SPIRIT!—WORKSHEET

"A fanatic is one who won't change his mind and won't change the subject."
—Winston Churchill

For discussion:

1. Can you choose to be enthusiastic or unenthusiastic? How can that choice make a difference in your performance?

_____

_____

_____

_____

_____

2. What do you think Harry Truman meant when he said, "Every great achievement is the story of a flaming heart."

_____

_____

_____

_____

_____

3. As a small group, develop a way to get your teammates enthusiastic right now!

_____

_____

_____

_____

Word of the Day: Fanatic—one who is excessively enthusiastic or devoted

IT'S A MATTER OF CHOICE—COACH'S NOTES

SAY: (5 MINUTES)

"It is not a matter of chance, rather a matter of choice. It is not a matter of something to be waited for, rather something to be gained." This statement was written by a man talking about how some people or groups of people are successful while others with the same ability are not. The statement says a great deal about "[Your School Name] Pride," its commitments, and its attitudes. Consider that statement, piece by piece.

❏ *IT IS NOT A MATTER OF CHANCE*

Luck has very little to do with success. People create their own luck. Nothing happens by chance. For something to happen, an action must be initiated by someone. Those people who wait for something to happen usually end up with the "coulda, woulda, shoulda" syndrome. Why does it appear that some teams have all the luck—always around to pick up the loose ball, catch the tipped ball, come back in the fourth quarter? Is it by chance?

❏ *IT IS A MATTER OF CHOICE*

People choose to be successful or unsuccessful. The greatest power that a person possesses is the power to choose. Every person has a choice to give his best or not give his best, to work hard or not work hard, to be committed or not be committed. You will make a choice in every practice and on every play, whether or not you choose to be successful. Some people choose to do what it takes to be successful, while losers blame it on chance. Your destiny is in your hands. If you and your teammates choose to do your best—to not accept defeat—you will be successful. Your actions will speak clearly as to what choice you have made. Anything less than full-speed effort is not your best. Your choice is your power to be in control of your destiny.

❏ *IT IS NOT A MATTER OF SOMETHING TO BE WAITED FOR, RATHER SOMETHING TO BE GAINED*

Your goal will not come to you—it is a matter of you going out and gaining it. You will get back exactly what you put in. You cannot wait to see if it will happen. You must make it happen. You be the catalyst; you be the cause. You be the one to make things happen. You be the one that leads. Do not wait for someone else to make it happen. Believe it will happen only if you make it happen. You will make things happen by your persistence of effort from the start of play to the very end; by your determination to do your best each play; by your concentration and enthusiasm; and by the habits you have developed through the choices you make.

DO: (15 MINUTES)

- Lead the group in a discussion of the questions found on the student worksheet.
- Review the word of the day. Ask a student to use it correctly in a sentence.

IT'S A MATTER OF CHOICE—WORKSHEET

"Indecision has often given an advantage to the other fellow because he did his thinking beforehand."

—Maurice Suritzen

For discussion:

1. "It is not a matter of chance, rather a matter of choice." Explain in your own words what you believe this statement means.

_____

_____

_____

_____

2. List some choices and their corresponding results.

   Examples: *Choosing to go to bed late will result in being tired the next day.*
   Choosing to study hard will result in good grades.

   Choosing to…   Will result in…

_____

_____

_____

_____

_____

3. Who has the power to choose?

_____

Word of the Day: Indecision—a wavering between two or more possible courses of action

WHAT ABOUT ME?—COACH'S NOTES

SAY: (5 MINUTES)

The team concept is a difficult thing to understand and accept for some athletes. It is human nature to be selfish, to always think, "What's in it for me?" You have to work at being unselfish. The most difficult thing for individuals to do when they are part of a team is to sacrifice. It's so easy to become selfish in a team environment—to play for *me*. It's make you very vulnerable to drop your guard and say, "This is who I am and I'm going to open up and give of myself to you." But that's exactly what you have to do. Willing sacrifice is the great paradox. Zig Ziglar says it like this: "You can have everything in life you want if you will just help enough other people get what they want."

Placing team goals ahead of individual goals defines the team concept. Every winning team has it and every losing team does not. An individual must unselfishly sacrifice his own personal wants and wishes for the good of the team.

Players must learn to cooperate and respect each other and build each other up. They must be interested in helping and improving each other. Team spirit and morale are developed by this process. When you have a group of young people working hard together for a common goal, you are tough to beat.

A few days before the Super Bowl, Assistant Head Coach Richie Petitbon tried to put his finger on what made the 1991 Washington Redskins unique. "This tends to be a selfish game, full of selfish stars," Petitbon explained, "but every once in a while a ball club gets totally caught up in the team concept. Egos get submerged. Everything is done for the good of the group."

Such was the case with the Redskins, Super Bowl champions after Sunday's 37-24 smashing of the Buffalo Bills. "This team really had great, great chemistry," Coach Joe Gibbs said. "The players had a great, great feeling for one another. From day one, I rarely got upset with our team. I very rarely had to deal with the off-the-field stuff. It was truly a team. It was not just a bunch of stars."

The following poem points out how selfishness can destroy. You all must learn that you have to give up something in the immediate to attract something even better in the future. Without sacrifice you'll never know your full potential.

The Cold Within

Six men were trapped by circumstance in bleak and bitter cold
Each one possessed a stick of wood, or so the story's told.
The dying fire in need of logs, the first man held his back
Because of faces 'round the fire, he noticed one was black.

The second man saw not one of his own local church
And couldn't bring himself to give the first his stick of birch.
The poor man sat in tattered clothes and gave his coat a hitch.
Why should he give up his log to warm the idle rich?

The rich man sat and thought of all the wealth he had in store
And how to keep what he had earned from the lazy, shiftless poor.
The black man's face spoke revenge and the fire passed from his sight,
Because he saw in his stick of wood a chance to spite the white.

The last man of this forlorn group did naught except for gain,
Only to those who gave to him was how he played the game.
Their logs held tight in death's still hands was proof of human sin.
They didn't die from cold without, they died from The Cold Within.

—Author Unknown

DO: (15 MINUTES)

- Discuss the questions on the student worksheet. Be sure to elicit specific suggestions from the team regarding the answer to Question #3.
- Review the word of the day. Ask a student to use it correctly in a sentence.

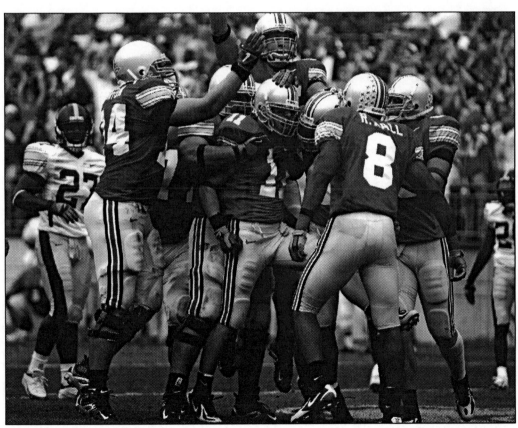

Photo Credit: Harry How/Getty Images Sport

WHAT ABOUT ME?—WORKSHEET

"Deferred joys purchased by sacrifice are always the sweetest."

—Mike Doyle

For discussion:

1. What is the most important lesson you can learn from the poem, "The Cold Within"?

_____

_____

_____

_____

2. How can you put this lesson to work in your life today?

_____

_____

_____

_____

3. What can you do as a team to help you remember the importance of teamwork?

_____

_____

_____

_____

Word of the Day: Sacrifice—to suffer loss, give up, renounce, or injure for an ideal, belief, or end

SELF-EVALUATION—COACH'S NOTES

SAY: (10 MINUTES)

It is important to examine the seven attitudes that help make up a winner. Listen to the descriptions carefully, because you will be asked to rate yourself on each of these traits.

❑ *DRIVE, DETERMINATION, OR DESIRE*

Jack Youngblood, an NFL linebacker, once said, "You learn that, whatever you are doing in life, obstacles don't matter very much. Pain or other circumstances can be there, but if you want to do a job badly enough, you will find a way to get it done."

This attitude trait can be defined as the enjoyment of facing a challenge and the need to win. The athlete who possesses this trait to a high degree looks forward to stiff competition, sets very high goals for himself, and aspires to be the best. He is quite willing to endure unpleasant things if he thinks it will help him succeed.

An example of a high degree of determination, drive, and desire can be found in the all-consuming interest in athletics expressed by some individuals. More than anything else, a driven athlete desires success and spends much of his time working toward his goals. He will challenge the toughest opponent. He gets a great deal of enjoyment out of competition. He is noticeably bothered after losing.

An athlete who rates low in this trait shows little interest in working toward goals. Athletics may be a pleasant pastime for him, but he can "take it or leave it"; goals just are not that important. This athlete avoids the tough opponent and does not take practice seriously.

At this point, on your worksheet, rate yourself on drive.

❑ *AGGRESSIVENESS—ATTACK THE OBJECTIVE*

Boxer Sugar Ray Robinson once remarked, "If you want to see a great fighter at his best, watch him when he is getting licked."

Aggression may be defined as the enjoyment of taking charge physically. An aggressive athlete is very concerned about not getting pushed around. He loves physical contact and is very anxious to get back at people who beat him. This kind of athlete makes things happen by carrying the battle to the opponent; he sets the tempo; he does not sit back and wait for things to happen.

A high degree of aggression is apparent in the athlete who seeks out the roughest opponent and concentrates on beating him. He is usually in the middle of rough play and shows no fear of being hurt. On the other hand, a person who is low in aggression is intimidated or frightened by a tough opponent. He shows no desire to challenge him, and he often gives up easily. He shies away from rough play.

At this point, on your worksheet, rate yourself on aggressiveness.

❏ *DEDICATION*

Walt Disney once observed, "All our dreams can come true if we have the courage and dedication to pursue them."

The person with dedication does not give up easily. He is willing to practice long and hard to achieve his goals. He is probably the first to practice and the last to leave. He spends extra time working on his skills by himself, sometimes to the point of exhaustion. No matter how many things go wrong, this person sticks to his goals, regardless of the cost in terms of time and effort.

You will recognize a dedicated athlete as consistently the hardest worker in practice. He never "eases up," and continues to work very hard regardless of the length of the practice. He is one of the last to quit and volunteers for extra work.

At the other extreme, the player low in dedication rarely spends extra time working on his skills. He is content to slide by on what he has without ever extending himself or putting in extra time. He gives up easily and uses excuses to get out of practice.

At this point, on your worksheet, rate yourself on dedication.

❏ *LEADERSHIP*

The athlete who possesses this characteristic likes to persuade his teammates to go the extra mile. He enjoys the opportunity to lead his teammates and is usually good at motivating the team. He likes to make decisions, is quite outspoken, and is often put in charge of things. He has an obvious willingness to put his ability on the line when facing others and he shows concern about the performances of his teammates. He is quite interested in interacting with his teammates to improve the overall team.

A high degree of leadership is apparent in the player who is able to motivate others when preparing for a big game. Others look to him because he seems to be able to provide them with the boost they need. He takes time to help other players. He is willing to take responsibility for teaching, communicating, and motivating teammates.

The person low in this trait may be described as a loner. He does not seem to be interested in relating to others and he rarely provides encouragement to teammates. He seems to be only interested in himself and rarely takes time to help others.

At this point, on your worksheet, rate yourself on leadership.

❏ *SELF-CONFIDENCE*

Excuse Dizzy Dean's grammar and listen to his words: "If you can do it, it ain't braggin'...it's a matter of con-fee-dence. I got where I did because I wasn't no shrinkin' violet."

The athlete with self-confidence is very sure of himself and his ability. He is not prone to worry about his play, to show indecisiveness, or to be upset by unexpected situations. He not only accepts criticism well from the coach, but also is very likely to speak up for what he believes, both to the coach and to the other players. This player eagerly anticipates the opportunity to display his ability. No doubt exists in this player's mind when preparing for a superior opponent; he knows he can defeat his adversary and he shows no regard for his reputation. He handles unexpected situations well. He voices a positive belief about his ability and makes decisions quickly and easily.

On the other hand, a player low in self-confidence always seems worried about the chances for disaster. He is more concerned with the possibility of, and effect of, a loss than with the advantage of a win. He gives up early against superior opponents and has difficulty making decisions.

At this point, on your worksheet, rate yourself on self-confidence.

❏ EMOTIONAL CONTROL

A person who can control his emotions is mature and stable. He is not likely to be adversely affected by his feelings. Quite often, his feelings do not even show. He is not easily depressed or frustrated by bad breaks, bad calls by the official, or by his own mistakes. A great deal of self-discipline is evident in this person's behavior. He rarely loses his temper and almost never feels picked on by other people.

Bart Starr, the NFL Hall of Famer, certainly displayed emotional control. He said, "A person can't brood over one mistake, or waste time feeling sorry for himself, or take on any sort of persecution complex…Today I realize that once you have made a mistake, you must accept it, profit by it, and then totally dismiss it from your mind."

In times of great stress, a player under emotional control is able to remain completely "cool" and seemingly unconcerned by the other team's success. He thinks clearly in critical situations. On the other hand, a player low in emotional control, when beaten once by his opponent, is through for the rest of the day. He simply can't recover and the other team focuses on him and destroys him. He is often moody. He gets very upset over a poor performance.

At this point, on your worksheet, rate yourself on emotional control.

❏ MENTAL TOUGHNESS

The athlete who is mentally tough is somewhat insensitive to the feelings and problems of others. He rarely gets upset when losing, playing badly, or being spoken to harshly. He is able to accept strong criticism without being hurt, and does not require too much encouragement from the coach to be effective. This person does not depend on the team for a sense of belonging.

When a mentally tough player receives harsh handling, is yelled at by the coach, or becomes the object of severe criticism, he seems to become even better or tougher. It seems sometimes to be the motivation he needs to make him perform at his best. He bounces back after being beaten and looks forward to a return match with the opponent. On the other hand, when a player is not mentally tough and receives harsh handling, he is quite likely to crawl into a shell and feel sorry for himself. He is ready to admit that he is "no good" and give up. He performs poorly after criticism. He does not recover well from a loss.

At this point, on your worksheet, rate yourself on mental toughness.

DO: (10 MINUTES)

- After the description of each trait, pause and let the students confidentially rate themselves.
- Discuss the questions on the student worksheet.
- Review the word of the day. Ask a student to use it correctly in a sentence.

Photo Credit: Andy Lyons/Getty Images Sport

SELF-EVALUATION—WORKSHEET

"A hero is no braver than an ordinary man, but he is brave five minutes longer."
—Ralph Waldo Emerson

Rate yourself in the seven attitude traits by circling the appropriate level:

Drive:	Low	Below Average	Average	Above Average	High
Aggressiveness:	Low	Below Average	Average	Above Average	High
Dedication:	Low	Below Average	Average	Above Average	High
Leadership:	Low	Below Average	Average	Above Average	High
Self-Confidence:	Low	Below Average	Average	Above Average	High
Emotional Control:	Low	Below Average	Average	Above Average	High
Mental Toughness:	Low	Below Average	Average	Above Average	High

For discussion:

1. List the three attitude traits in which you rated yourself the highest. What can you do to use these traits to promote your best performance?

_____

_____

_____

_____

2. List the three attitude traits in which you rated yourself the lowest. What actions can you take to improve yourself in these three attitude traits?

_____

_____

_____

_____

Word of the Day: Heroism—to have traits that are admired or to show great courage

HOPE—COACH'S NOTES

LESSON #11

SAY: (5 MINUTES)

Hope is an important ingredient of persistence. If a person has hope in the future, he has power in the present.

Consider the following story of a boy who found hope:Little Ben Hooper was born at a time when if you didn't know who your father was, you were ostracized from society. When Ben started school, he would stay inside by himself at recess. He brought his lunch and always ate alone. When he and his mother would go to the general store on Saturday to get groceries, the self-righteous ladies would say in a whisper you could hear about 200 yards away, "I wonder if he knows who his father is. I wonder if she knows." Little Ben seemed to be sentenced to a life of loneliness and despair. Then he heard about a new young preacher. Ben and his mom did not go to church, but all the kids were talking about the new preacher, so little Ben decided to go.

The church had a ritual at the end of the service; one of the members would pray and the preacher would go to the back of the church and shake hands with each person. For the first time in his young life, little Ben was hopeful. On this particular Sunday, the preacher seemed to be talking right to Ben. He said it didn't matter where you had been; all that mattered was where you were going. Before little Ben knew it, they were praying and the preacher was at the back of the church. Ben tried to mingle with the crowd and suddenly felt a hand on his shoulder. When he turned he was looking into the eyes of the preacher.

The young preacher asked the question everyone had wanted to ask publicly for years: "Whose boy are you?" You could have heard the proverbial pin drop. Then the young preacher smiled and said, "Why it is obvious whose child you are. The resemblance is remarkable. You are a child of God. Now go and claim the inheritance you so richly deserve." Little Ben Hooper later said that was the day he was elected Governor of Tennessee and later re-elected. That day he went from being the son of an unknown father to being the song of a King. That day he was given hope in the future, which gave him the persistence to achieve his success.

DO: (15 MINUTES)

- Lead a discussion from the questions on the student worksheet. Be sure to let the students do the talking and always ask for specific examples.
- Review the word of the day. Ask a student to use it correctly in a sentence.

HOPE—WORKSHEET

"It wasn't raining when Noah started building the Ark."

—Unknown

For discussion:

1. Describe one situation in your life when persistence paid off for you or someone you know.

_____

_____

_____

_____

_____

2. How do you find hope when it is sometimes difficult?

_____

_____

_____

_____

_____

3. What do you gain by being persistent? By quitting?

_____

_____

_____

_____

Word of the Day: Hope—to desire with expectation of obtainment

ABRAHAM LINCOLN—COACH'S NOTES

SAY: (5 MINUTES)

If you want to learn about somebody who didn't quit, Abraham Lincoln is probably the greatest example. Abraham Lincoln could have quit many times. Because he chose not to, he became one of the greatest presidents in the history of the United States. Lincoln was a true warrior and exemplified the word champion. Consider this list of side trips on Lincoln's road to the White House:

1831 – Failed in business
1832 – Defeated for the Legislature
1833 – Second failure in business
1836 – Suffered nervous breakdown
1838 – Defeated for Speaker of the House
1840 – Defeated for Elector
1843 – Defeated for Congress
1848 – Defeated for Senate
1856 – Defeated for Vice-President
1858 – Defeated for Senate
1860 – Elected President of the United States

"The path is worn and slippery. My foot slipped from under me, knocking the other out of the way," Lincoln said, after losing a Senate race. "But I recovered and said to myself, 'it's a slip and not a fall.'"

The adversity (or struggle) is what gave Abraham Lincoln the character to lead the United States to victory during its most difficult time. Lincoln stated, "I am a slow walker, but I never walk back."

DO: (15 MINUTES)

- Lead a discussion from the questions on the student worksheet. Be sure to let the students do the talking and always ask for specific examples.
- Review the word of the day. Ask a student to use it correctly in a sentence.

ABRAHAM LINCOLN—WORKSHEET

"Failure is only the opportunity to begin again more intelligently."

—Dennis Parker

For discussion:

1. Why do you think Abraham Lincoln was able to endure all the failures and keep running for office? Consider this quote in your answer: "The sense of obligation to continue is present in all of us. A duty to strive is the duty of us all. I felt a call of that duty."

_____

_____

_____

_____

2. How can learning of Lincoln's failures help you?

_____

_____

_____

_____

3. How did the failures in Lincoln's life prepare him for the job of leading a nation during the Civil War?

_____

_____

_____

_____

Word of the Day: Opportunity—a good chance for advancement or progress

HELPING OTHERS MEANS HELPING YOURSELF— COACH'S NOTES

SAY: (5 MINUTES)

Zig Ziglar once said, "You can have everything in life you want if you will just help enough other people get what they want."

A wonderful law of nature states that three of the things people desire most in life—happiness, freedom, and peace of mind—can be attained when they are given to others. "The more we give, the more we have."

Consider the following story, which teaches the importance of helping others: Sadu was a missionary to India. Late on afternoon, Sadu was traveling on foot through the Himalayas with a Buddhist monk. It was bitterly cold and the wind felt like sharp blades slicing into Sadu's skin. Night was fast approaching when the monk warned Sadu they were in danger of freezing to death if they did not reach the monastery before darkness fell. Just as they were traversing a narrow path above a steep precipice, they heard a cry for help. Down the cliff lay a man who had fallen and was badly hurt. The monk looked at Sadu and warned him not to stop. The monk believed God had brought this man to his fate and he must work it out for himself. He hurried his step as he passed the gentleman.

Sadu replied, "God has sent me here to help my brother. I cannot abandon him." The monk continued trudging off through the whirling snow while Sadu clambered down the steep embankment. The man's leg was broken and he could not walk. Sadu took his blanket, made a sling out of it, and tied the man to his back. Bending under his burden, he began a body-torturing climb. By the time he reached the narrow path again, he was drenched in perspiration. Doggedly, he made his path through the deepening snow and darkness. It was all he could do to follow the path. Though faint with fatigue and overheated with exertion, he finally saw the lights of the monastery ahead. For the first time Sadu stumbled and nearly fell, but not from weakness. He stumbled upon an object lying under the snow. Slowly he bent down on one knee and brushed the snow off the object. It was the body of the monk, frozen to death. Later Sadu would learn that the reason he had not suffered the same fate as the monk was that the body heat generated by the man he carried had probably saved his life. He had lived because he had risked his life.

DO: (15 MINUTES)

*   Lead a discussion from the questions on the student worksheet. Be sure to let the students do the talking and always ask for specific examples.
*   Review the word of the day. Ask a student to use it correctly in a sentence.

HELPING OTHERS MEANS HELPING YOURSELF— WORKSHEET

"If there is a why in your life, the how does not matter."

—Friedrich Nietzsche

For discussion:

1. Why is it true that when you give some gifts away, you end up receiving them also?

_____

_____

_____

_____

2. What actions do you take in your daily life that reflect the monk's attitude?

_____

_____

_____

_____

3. How can you reflect Sadu's attitude in your daily life?

_____

_____

_____

_____

Word of the Day: Help—to give assistance or support

FAITH: UNQUESTIONING BELIEF—COACH'S NOTES

SAY: (5 MINUTES)

Faith is never a complete quality; faith is a precedent to something else. If you have faith, you will do something. The word "believing" can be more accurately spelled "be-living." If you have faith and if you believe tobacco is unhealthy, you would "be-living" without using tobacco. If you have faith and if you believe that premarital sex is mentally, physically, and emotionally dangerous, you would "be-living" in celibacy before marriage. If you have faith in something, your walk (the way you live) will mirror your talk.

In the early 20th century, a young man in Albany, New York, posted notices all through town declaring that on Saturday morning, he would walk across a canyon pushing a wheelbarrow on nothing but a cable. Many people in the town came out due to curiosity. Before the man started across the canyon, he asked the people how many thought he could push the wheelbarrow across the cable. Just a few replied, "We think you can." Without hesitation, the young man deftly pushed the wheelbarrow across the canyon. When he was on the other side he yelled across and asked the people if they thought he could push the wheelbarrow back across. The entire crowd yelled in unison, "We know you can." The young man asked, "Who will ride in the wheelbarrow?"

You must have enough faith to get in the wheelbarrow. Your faith will sometimes be doubted and tested. Research everything. Once you determine something is worthy of your faith, be willing to take a risk and believe it will get you through.

DO: (15 MINUTES)

- Lead a discussion from the questions on the student worksheet. Be sure to let the students do the talking and always ask for specific examples.
- Review the word of the day. Ask a student to use it correctly in a sentence.

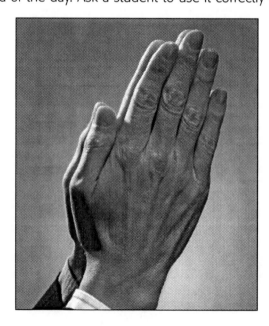

FAITH: UNQUESTIONING BELIEF—WORKSHEET

"Do not fear to step into the unknown. For where there is risk, there is also reward."
—Lori Hard

For discussion:

1. What does "faith" mean to you?

_____

_____

_____

_____

2. When in your life have you had to have faith?

_____

_____

_____

3. How does lack of faith destroy a person or group?

_____

_____

_____

_____

4. How do you gain faith?

_____

_____

_____

Word of the Day: Believe—to accept as true, genuine, or real, or to have a firm conviction as to the goodness, efficacy, or ability of something

HUMOR: ABILITY AND WILLINGNESS TO LAUGH— COACH'S NOTES

SAY: (5 MINUTES)

More than 30 years ago, Norman Cousins was dying in a hospital room at UCLA Medical Center. Doctors told him his disease was terminal and that nothing could be done. Cousins would not accept their diagnosis. One night after watching a Marx Brothers movie on television, he laughed so hard it exhausted him and he slept soundly without narcotics for the first time in weeks. After this discovery, he ordered in a film projector and all the Marx Brothers' movies and slapstick comedy he could get his hands on. He noticed immediate health improvements. The pain decreased to a tolerable level, he slept soundly, and amazingly, blood tests showed that his immune system was healing and the inflammation went down. Cousins went on to chronicle his recovery in the highly acclaimed book *Anatomy of an Illness*, published in 1969. This book is viewed as a cornerstone of Humor Therapy.

Stress has been cited as a contributing factor in disease. Some figures go as far as saying that 80 percent of all disease is due to stress. Humor is certainly one way to release and cope with stress. You can't laugh and hold on to a blue mood for very long.

Laughter can improve circulation. When people laugh, skin temperature increases. Laughter also lowers blood pressure, stabilizes the heart rate, and can change blood chemistry. Laughter has been shown to increase blood oxygen levels, which in itself can be a healing event. It also reduces tension.

Dr. Lee Bark, a medical researcher and professor, found that laughter lowers the pressure of cortisol in the bloodstream. Cortisol is a derivation of cortices steroids that appears when a system is under stress. It has been shown to interfere with the proper function of the immune system.

Other positive results can also occur with laughter. For example, a person's immune system is boosted. T-cell and multicell production is elevated when blood-cell activity is increased. According to documented research, laughing increases the production of other elemental immune system cells and gamin interferon, both of which can help fight cancer.

Endorphins, which are natural painkillers, also increase with laughter. In fact, 10 different muscle groups are exercised when a person laughs. They contract and relax and, in a very real way, perform a sort of visceral massage on the internal organs.

In a study conducted by Stanford University researchers, catheters were plugged into college students and the study participants were made to watch funny movies. The subsequent laughter of the participants caused their white blood cell activity to increase immediately. The key point that should be noted is that laughter and a sense of humor are good for you.

DO: (15 MINUTES)

- Lead a discussion from the questions on the student worksheet. Be sure to let the students do the talking and always ask for specific examples.
- Review the word of the day. Ask a student to use it correctly in a sentence.

LESSON #15

LESSON #15: HUMOR: ABILITY AND WILLINGNESS TO LAUGH—WORKSHEET

"Humor is by far the most significant activity of the human brain."

—Edward De Bond

For discussion:

1. What does "humor" mean to you?

_____

_____

_____

_____

2. The average five-year-old child laughs 500 times a day, and the average adult 18 times a day. Why?

_____

_____

_____

3. How does having a sense of humor affect the way you see things?

_____

_____

_____

4. If laughter is so important to health, why is it not used more as a therapy?

_____

_____

_____

Word of the Day: Heal—to restore to health, or to cause an undesirable condition to be overcome

RESPONSIBILITY

Chapter 3

"What we are born with is God's gift to us. What we do with it is our gift to God."

—Anonymous

IF IT'S GOING TO BE, IT'S UP TO ME—
COACH'S NOTES

Say: (5 minutes)

Why would responsibility be the first thing you need to learn?

Situation: The team loses the game and your dad says the coach called the wrong play.

Logic: The team can only win if the coach calls a perfect game. Team success is totally up to the coach's play calling.

Fact: During the course of a game, a coach will, on the average, call 10 bad plays. The players have to prevent disaster on these plays. On the other hand, the coach will call 10 plays that should be big plays. When one of these is called, the players have to make it happen. In between are the other 40 plays.

Situation: A student fails a class. His response is, "The teacher did not teach me."

Logic: If I do not have a good teacher and he does not do a great job of teaching, then I will fail. In other words, your academic success depends upon how good your teachers are. Are the books used by the bad teacher the same as those used by the good teacher?

Fact: All teachers use the same books. Information is available. The responsibility to get information is yours.

Situation: The team loses the game. They feel the referee cheated them by making a bad call, so it is his fault the team lost.

Logic: The team can only win if calls go
its way.

Fact: The team cannot overcome human mistakes by referees. In other words, team success is dictated by referees.

Situation: The team loses a game in the rain and blames the weather.

Logic: The team can only win if the weather is right.

Fact: Team success is dependent upon good weather.

Who is responsible for your success or failure? Until you accept responsibility, what is your hope? Can you change the referees, teachers, coaches, or weather? Until you accept responsibility for your success and the team accepts responsibility for its success, no hope exists. As long as it is other people's fault that the team is not winning, no hope for improvement exists either.

Can you change the way you were raised? Can you change the coach? Can you change or improve the referees? Always keep in mind that you are responsible for you. Improve you, and you will improve everything.

A father was busy doing a report. His young son kept bothering him with questions. Finally the father took a picture of the world from a magazine, tore it into pieces and told his young son to piece it back together as a puzzle. He thought that would keep the boy busy. When the young boy returned a few minutes later the dad was curious as to how he could have pieced the world together so quickly. "It was easy," the boy said, "On the back of the world picture was a picture of a man, and when I got him straight, the world was straight."

When you get yourself straight, the world will be right.

Do: (15 minutes)

- Allow three to five minutes for the students to individually answer Questions #1 and #2. Then, discuss their answers as a large group.
- Spend five minutes discussing in small work groups or as a big group the answers to Question #3. Give any coping techniques you have.
- As the students answer Question #4, you may want them to commit by telling the entire team or finding one other person on the team with whom to share their answer.
- Review the word of the day. Ask a student to use it correctly in a sentence.

Photo Credit: Donald Miralle/Getty Images Sport

LESSON #1

IF IT'S GOING TO BE, IT'S UP TO ME—WORKSHEET

"He who sacrifices his conscience to ambition burns a picture to obtain the ashes."
—Chinese Proverb

For discussion:

1. What are some things in your life over which you have no control?

   _____

   _____

   _____

2. What are some things in your life over which you do have control?

   _____

   _____

   _____

3. How can the things you listed in Question #2 help you cope with the things you listed in Question #1?

   _____

   _____

   _____

4. What is one thing you can take more responsibility for (something you can control) that will improve your life and help your team?

   _____

   _____

   _____

Word of the Day: Conscience—awareness of right and wrong

IN SPITE OF THE WEATHER—COACH'S NOTES

Say: (5 minutes)

When the Alaskan Pipeline was being built, many Texans went to Alaska and found work on the pipeline. The Texans could only work a few hours in the frigid weather, yet the Eskimos, the native Alaskans, could work indefinitely in the cold. Scientists decided to do a study to find out why the Eskimos could withstand the weather. They found that no physiological differences existed between the Eskimos and the Texans. Nothing in terms of skin thickness, blood, or any other physical aspect would explain the differences in the ability to withstand the cold. The solution came when scientists did a psychological study. One Eskimo said, "I knew it was cold but there was a job to be done." In other words, his focus was on the job and obtaining results, rather than on the weather. The Texans tended to focus on the weather, which kept them from focusing on the job at hand.

You are responsible for performing. Your focus must be on the job. You are to be results-oriented. When you go to practice in August, it will be hot. When you play in December, it will be cold. The team will likely play in the rain or even snow. You are responsible to perform. You are responsible to focus on performance, not the weather.

Weather cannot dictate performance. As proud as you are to be [Your School's Mascot], your attitude to athletic performance has to be that of the Eskimos. Irregardless of whether it is hot, cold, or wet, you should always focus on your job, not the weather.

Do: (15 minutes)

- Lead the class in a discussion of the questions on the student worksheet. Spend a considerable amount of time on Question #1 to generate many ideas from the team.
- Review the word of the day. Ask a student to use it correctly in a sentence.

LESSON #2

IN SPITE OF THE WEATHER—WORKSHEET

"He who is the most slow in making a promise is the most faithful in the performance of it."

—Jean-Jacques Rousseau

For discussion:

1. How do you become "Eskimos"?

_____

_____

_____

_____

2. Why is this so important to your success?

_____

_____

_____

_____

3. Who is responsible to see that this happens?

_____

_____

_____

_____

Word of the Day: Perform—to begin and carry out, to accomplish

IN SPITE OF CIRCUMSTANCES—COACH'S NOTES

Say: (5 minutes)

One week, a player was removed from a team because he habitually missed practice and on the few occasions that he did practice, he performed poorly and was a detriment to the team. He lacked physical ability, mental toughness, and was spiritually void, as best as could be ascertained by his actions. He appealed, saying he felt he was losing his role because he was black.

During the same week, a man was complaining so much so that his pessimism would have made him an excellent "cruise director on the Titanic." He had nothing good to say to, or about, anyone. He complained that he was in a dead-end job, but that he would have received several promotions if he had been black or a woman.

In the first case, the young football player felt he was cheated of his rightful place because he was black. In the other, the man felt he was cheated of his rightful place because he was not black. Unfortunately, unless these two people change their attitudes, they will always be "left out" because they are or are not black—a circumstance that they will never be able to change. As long as such an excuse is given, they will never have to acknowledge their own weaknesses as reasons for their failure.

People always want to use circumstances as reasons for not succeeding. On the list of the 300 greatest leaders (which includes Helen Keller, Martin Luther King, Mahatma Gandhi, and Franklin Roosevelt), 75 were born in abject poverty, were abused as children, or suffered with a severe physical handicap. These people did not allow circumstance to prevent them from being successful. Supreme Court Justice Oliver Wendell Holmes, who was only five feet tall, once said, when asked how it felt to be so short, "I think it would be like a dime when thrown in with a bunch of nickels—half as small, worth twice as much." Circumstances do not dictate personal or team success. Your socioeconomic status, your color, your past history (or the team's) are the only indications of where you begin. You and only you are responsible for where you finish.

Do: (15 minutes)

- Lead a discussion on Questions #1–3. On Question #2, ask for specific stories. These stories can be inspiring to the team.
- Question #4 can be answered individually with no one sharing the answers aloud. If you have time, you may ask for volunteers to share.
- Review the word of the day. Ask a student to use it correctly in a sentence.

LESSON #3

IN SPITE OF CIRCUMSTANCES—WORKSHEET

"When we are flat on our backs there is no way to look but up."

—Roger W. Babson

For discussion:

1. What are circumstances you hear about that people use as causes for failure?

   _____

   _____

   _____

2. Has anyone ever overcome them?

   _____

   _____

   _____

3. Why is this important to know?

   _____

   _____

   _____

4. What are some excuses you may have used in the past? Can you overcome them?

   _____

   _____

   _____

Word of the Day: Despair—to lose all hope

GETTING RID OF THE "LOSER'S LIMP"— COACH'S NOTES

LESSON #4

Say: (5 minutes)

Failure to accept responsibility is as old as time itself. To paraphrase a story from Genesis: After Adam and Eve had eaten from the tree even after God had forbidden them to do so, God was looking for Adam in the Garden where Adam was hiding. When God found Adam, Adam blamed the woman. When God talked to Eve, she blamed the snake. The poor snake did not have a leg to stand on.

It is always something or someone else's fault. Zig Ziglar calls this phenomenon a "loser's limp." Have you ever been to a track meet and watched the runners in the 400-meter dash? They all take off with high hopes and sprint to win. As the race progresses, one runner will notice that he does not have a chance to win and very easily could end up in last place. That is when he begins to "limp," usually with a "pulled hamstring." The crowd thinks, "Why of course he can't win—he is injured," when many times it is simply a crutch to prevent the athlete from facing the loss.

Ziglar tells the story of the defensive back beaten on a deep pass. When the defender realized he was not going to catch the receiver, he came up with the convenient "loser's limp."

You may have seen it more often when a player acts as if something is "unimportant." He acts like he doesn't care if he wins, makes first team, or gets named All-District. This response is the "mental loser's limp." If he acted as if it were important and meant something and then does not get it, he would risk losing face with his peers.

Do: (15 minutes)

- Divide the team into small work groups and allow them 10 minutes to complete the three questions.
- Have each team share the highlights of the discussion or assign each small group a particular question on which to report.
- Review the word of the day. Ask a student to use it correctly in a sentence.

GETTING RID OF THE "LOSER'S LIMP"—
WORKSHEET

"Keep true, never be ashamed of doing right; decide on what you think is right and stick to it."

—George Eliot

For discussion:

1. Give examples of "loser's limps" that you have seen. They can be both physical and mental ones.

   _____

   _____

   _____

2. Why is it important to overcome a "loser's limp"?

   _____

   _____

   _____

3. What, if any, are some "loser's limps" your team has?

   _____

   _____

   _____

4. How can the team overcome its "loser's limps"?

   _____

   _____

   _____

Word of the Day: Integrity—strict adherence to a standard of value or conduct

LEARNING TO RESPOND, NOT REACT, TO LIFE— COACH'S NOTES

Say: (5 minutes)

Consider the following points concerning the need to respond, rather than react to life.

You go to a doctor, and he prescribes a medicine and tells you to come back in a few days. If, when you return to the doctor, he says, "Oh, no! You are having a *reaction* to the medicine, we need to change the prescription," that is bad. If, however, when you return, the doctor says, "Oh, good! Your body is *responding* to the medicine," that is good!

It is not what happens to you that causes you to succeed or fail. It is how you respond. For examplee, a player strikes out, throws his bat, kicks the bench, turns over the water cooler, and stomps into the dugout. Is he reacting or responding? The response to striking out is to calmly put all of the equipment up and stay in control of your emotions. After the game, take extra batting practice to prevent the strikeout from happening again.

The following story, by Zig Ziglar, illustrates the difference between responding and reacting. We pulled into the airport at exactly two o'clock. There were two long lines. We selected the shortest of the two. I noticed almost immediately that one of the ticket agents was walking around behind the counter, and I saw a *position closed* sign at one end. My experience told me she would remove *position closed* and replace it with *position open*, so I mentally and physically got ready to make a quick dash to the counter when she opened the other line. In a matter of minutes she walked over to the *position closed* sign, flipped it to *position open*, and smilingly announced to the group, "The three o'clock flight to Dallas has been cancelled." To this, I enthusiastically responded, "Fantastic!" When I said that, the ticket agent, with a puzzled expression on her face, asked, "Now, why in the world would you say 'fantastic' when I've just told you the three o'clock flight to Dallas has been cancelled?" I smiled back at her and said, "Ma'am, there are only three reasons why anybody would cancel a flight to Dallas, Texas. Number one, something must be wrong with that airplane; number two, something must be wrong with the person who is going to fly that airplane; number three, something must be wrong with the weather they're going to fly that airplane in. Now, ma'am, if any one of these three situations exists, I don't want to be up there. I want to be right down here! Fantastic!"

Have you ever noticed how some people seem to delight in delivering bad news? It's as if they just can't wait to let you know that life is tough and you're in for a tough time. To my response, the ticket agent put her hands on her hips in an authoritative, "I'm not through with you yet" kind of position and said, "Yes, but the next flight doesn't leave until 6:05." To that I responded, "Fantastic!"

By now people in the other two lines were looking in my direction and undoubtedly wondering, "Who is that nut who says everything is fantastic?" The lady herself looked at me in complete shock and said, "Now I'm really puzzled. Why in the world would you say 'fantastic' when I've just told you that you've got a four-hour wait in the airport in Kansas City?" I smilingly said, "Ma'am, it's really very simple. Do you realize that at this moment there are literally tens of millions of people on the face of the earth who are not only cold, but who are also hungry? Here I am in a beautiful facility, and even though it's cold outside, it's comfortable inside. Down the corridor is a nice little coffee shop. I am going to go down there, relax for a few minutes, and enjoy a cup of coffee. Then I've got some extremely important work which I need to do, and here I am in one of the nicest buildings in the whole area. It is easily the biggest, most comfortable, rent-free office I've ever had at my disposal. Fantastic!"

You might wonder in your own mind if I really felt that way and the answer is no, I did not. I was tired, had been gone all week, and wanted to get home. However, there are some things in life you're not going to change. If you were born white, you're going to stay white. If you were born black, you're going to stay black. As a matter of fact, you cannot change when you were born, where you were born, how you were born, or to whom you were born. Actually, you can't change one whisper about yesterday, but tomorrow is an entirely different story and today is the same. Whether you respond, which is positive, or react, which is negative, to life will determine just how good the rest of your day and the rest of your tomorrows are going to be. When you respond, both will be better. When you react, you've just put a ceiling on what you're able to do with your life.

> *Note*: You may prefer to give a personal example that illustrates the difference between responding and reacting.

Do: (15 minutes)

- Divide the team into smaller work groups and give each group a situation from the list in Question #1 and have them develop a scene showing a possible "reaction" and a possible "response." You may have them just report back the response and reaction instead of role play. This method takes less time, but does not require as much creativity.
- Debrief the role plays by discussing Questions #2 and #3.
- Review the word of the day. Ask a student to use it correctly in a sentence.

LEARNING TO RESPOND, NOT REACT, TO LIFE— WORKSHEET

LESSON #5

"Confidence is that feeling by which the mind embarks in great and honorable courses with a sure hope and trust in itself."

—Cicero

For discussion:

1. With your team, brainstorm how you could react negatively or respond positively to your assigned situation from the list below. Be prepared to show a possible "reaction" and a possible "response" in a two-minute role play.
   - A fumble occurs
   - Your position changes
   - The team loses a game
   - A teacher incorrectly rebukes you
   - The opponent scores
   - Your girlfriend/boyfriend breaks up with you
   - The coach yells at you
   - You are demoted
   - Your parents are divorcing
   - You are thinking about quitting

2. What is the key to choosing to respond instead of react?

   _____

   _____

   _____

3. What are some of the possible consequences of choosing to react or respond to your assigned situation?

   _____

   _____

   _____

Word of the Day: Optimism—a disposition to expect the best possible outcome or to emphasize the most positive aspects of a situation

BUILDING A FOUNDATION—COACH'S NOTES

Say: (5 minutes)

Have you ever seen an old abandoned place that is nothing but grass and weeds? Only a few signs exist that a house or a structure of any kind had ever stood in that location. You wonder, "where is everything?" If you asked around you would find that the old house had no foundation. It was build on piers and beams and everything has rotted away.

Have you ever visited a construction site? In the beginning stages, the site is actually just a huge hole in the ground with walls all around to keep people out. If you were to stop and visit with a construction worker and ask why a huge hole is dug first, he would explain that you could tell the height of a building by the depth of the foundation. The higher you want to build a building, the deeper the foundation.

People are similar to buildings in that respect. As in the example of the old home, if no foundation exists, no memory of an existence will survive. In the second example, you will go as high as your foundation allows. The deeper and more solid your foundation, the higher you will go.

Everyone wants the same things. They want to be healthy, happy, reasonably prosperous, secure, and to have friends, peace of mind, good family relationships, and hope. For a person to have these things, his foundation must be built on the traits of faith, love, loyalty, character, honesty, integrity, commitment, perseverance, and persistence.

Setting the foundation is your responsibility. Input equals output. Whatever you put into your mind is what will come out. If you load your mind with garbage, it will produce garbage. If you pump into your mind the pure, the clean, the powerful, and the positive, out will come the pure, the clean, the powerful, and the positive. This input includes what you listen to, what you watch, and what you read. If you dream of going anywhere and leaving a mark to be remembered you must lay that strong foundation. You do this by reading positive books about people who have these qualities and by watching videos of people helping people. You look for people with these traits. It is your responsibility to lay the foundation.

Years ago, a town was growing toward what had been the city garbage dump. For years, people had taken their garbage and dropped it in the dump. Then the city started putting good dirt over the garbage. After many loads of dirt, the garbage was completely covered and a beautiful new shopping center was built on the site.

No matter what has been going on in your mind, it can be "covered" or replaced with good foundational material. It does not happen accidentally. You have to make the effort to put in the good and the powerful and the positive. It is your responsibility to lay the foundation.

Do: (15 minutes)

- Divide the group into three smaller work groups. Assign each group one question. After a discussion period, have the group leader report the answer.
- Review the word of the day. Ask a student to use it correctly in a sentence.

LESSON #6

BUILDING A FOUNDATION—WORKSHEET

"No race can prosper till it learns that there is as much dignity in tilling a field as in writing a poem."

—Booker T. Washington

For discussion:

1. What are you reading, listening to, and watching that will be your foundation?

    _____

    _____

    _____

    _____

2. What can you change to improve your foundation?

    _____

    _____

    _____

    _____

3. Give three specific examples of when input influenced the output.

    _____

    _____

    _____

    _____

Word of the Day: Dignity—state of being worthy or honored

CHOICES AND CONSEQUENCES—COACH'S NOTES

Say: (5 minutes)

How many of you believe that you are a product of the choices that you make each day?

If you choose to eat too much, you have made a conscious decision to be overweight. Being overweight is no accident. Nobody accidentally eats anything. You choose to eat the wrong things. You choose to be overweight.

If you choose to smoke a cigarette, you have chosen to die 14 minutes sooner. The choice is to use tobacco, and the consequence is to die 14 minutes sooner than you otherwise would have.

If you choose to not work out during the summer, you have chosen to put yourself at high risk of being injured during practice. Because you are injured, you cannot work out, so you remain in poor physical condition. When your injury is healed, you return to practice still in poor shape, only to be hurt again. It is not bad luck. It is a result of a choice you made when you decided to not work out during the summer.

When you choose to put chemicals into your body, you have chosen to destroy the chances you have for success. In athletics, your weapon is your body. When you choose to mistreat it, you have chosen to give yourself a poor chance for success.

Remember the old saying, "If you go to the dance, you have to pay the fiddler." In other words, for every choice you make, a consequence will follow.

Someone once told a story of being in an ice cream parlor when a young man and his girlfriend walked in. The young man had a hairstyle that looked like the reprieve came from the warden right after they plugged in the chair. His hair was sticking straight up in every color. Does this young man have the right to wear his hair in any fashion? Yes, of course. You can choose to wear your hair in any manner you wish, but when you do, you choose to eliminate a large percentage of people who might employ you.

Before you make a choice, always consider the consequences. You will find that you will make much better choices.

Do: (15 minutes)

- Lead a discussion of the questions found on the student worksheet.
- Review the word of the day. Ask a student to use it correctly in a sentence.

CHOICES AND CONSEQUENCES—WORKSHEET

"It is as hard to do your duty when men are sneering at you as when they are shooting at you."

—Woodrow Wilson

For discussion:

1. How do you choose your friends?

_____

_____

_____

_____

2. How do you choose your food?

_____

_____

_____

_____

3. What can you do to improve your choices?

_____

_____

_____

_____

Word of the Day: Duty—a moral or legal obligation

PLAY TO WIN—COACH'S NOTES

Say: (5 minutes)

Consider the following story of a football coach and reflect on its point about the importance of playing to win.

In 1983, he was on the coaching staff of the 5A Football State Champions. He left and took a head coaching position in a 5A school in East Texas. He was excited upon arrival, and even more excited when he discovered he had better athletes than at the state champion team he had just left.

With all that talent, how is it that they went 5-5 in 1984, 2-8 in 1985, and 4-6 in 1986? Needless to say, it was a very frustrating three years. He had tried everything in terms of motivating the athletes to perform.

At the conclusion of the 1986 season, he was having a conversation with one of his seniors. He was told, "Coach, you are never going to be happy here. You are coaching to win, we are playing to play. We will do whatever it takes to be a member of the team and to go to the pep rally and to play on Friday night, but we know there is no chance for us to win. No one has won here in many years, so we know to be satisfied with just being on the team."

That was the reason the team could look so good in practice and then look so miserable on game night. Once they ran through that "breakthrough," they had accomplished their goal. Getting on the field was the goal—not performing. They had such a tradition of not winning that they did not believe they could win They started that off-season with a new motto: "Play to win." It did not mean they had to win to be successful, but they had to "play to win"—in other words, to do everything possible to win the games. This simple motto was talked about every day.

One day one of the players said, "There are teachers who teach to teach, not to win." They do what is required to keep their jobs. It was a different classroom when the evaluation day arrived. Their goal was not to do their job but to keep their job.

The revelation was simple. People who "play to win" are happy and enjoy immensely what they do. It is the reason that so-called manual laborers may be happier than some affluent businessmen. They determined that it was not what you do that determines in your mind if you are successful. It is how you do what you do that determines your success.

They also determined that everyone defines failure in exactly the same way. That is, failure is the inability to reach whatever objective you set out to reach. On the other hand, success is defined differently by every individual. Whereas the previous team in the coach's story had defined success as the ability to play on Friday night, his new team defined success as the determination to play to win.

The 1987 team did indeed "play to win." They won eight ball games, the most that had been won by the city's team since 1966. More importantly, they laid the foundation for all future teams: that "playing to play" would not be tolerated nor accepted. To be on this team, you didn't have to win, but you did have to "play to win."

What is your responsibility as far as performance? It is not to win. Not everyone can win, but everyone can "play to win." You are responsible to do everything within your power physically, mentally, legally, and ethically to win every day you play. Once you do that, you are successful, no matter what the scoreboard says.

Do: (15 minutes)

- Divide the team into smaller work groups. Assign each group a situation for them to role play the different attitudes.
- After the role plays, discuss the questions found on the student worksheet.
- Review the word of the day. Ask a student to use it correctly in a sentence.

Photo Credit: Rick Stewart/Getty Images Sport

PLAY TO WIN—WORKSHEET

"The purpose of competition is not to beat someone down, but to bring out the best in every player."

—Amos Alonzo Stagg

For discussion:

1. Which of these two attitudes do you have—play to play, or play to win? What are some specific behaviors you exhibit that show this attitude in your life?

_____

_____

_____

_____

_____

_____

2. How do you become a team that "plays to win"?

_____

_____

_____

_____

_____

_____

_____

Word of the Day: Compete—to contend with another

LIVING A BUTTERFLY LIFE—COACH'S NOTES

Say: (5 minutes)

You are responsible "to live." What a silly thing to say! You don't need anyone to tell you to live. However, it is not as silly as you might think.

Theodore Roosevelt once was asked what his greatest desire was. He replied, "To live until I die." What did he mean by that? It seems nonsensical. Everyone will live until he dies. But try to look at it in a different way.

John Henry Fabre, the great French naturalist, conducted a most unusual experiment with processionary caterpillars. These caterpillars each blindly follow the one in front of them. Hence, the name "processionary." Fabre carefully arranged them in a circle around the rim of a flower pot, so that the lead caterpillar actually touched the last one, making a complete circle. In the center of the flower pot, he put pine needles, which is food for processionary caterpillars. The caterpillars started around this circular flower pot. Around and around they went, hour after hour, day after day, night after night. For seven full days and seven full nights they went around the flower pot. Finally, they dropped dead of starvation and exhaustion. With an abundance of food less than six inches away, they literally starved to death. With life six inches away, they died.

Inside each caterpillar is a "success instinct." In the caterpillar, it is simply a "survival and procreation instinct." Man has much more. Man has the ability to imagine, to see himself as anything he wants to be, to live any way he wants. To live, to man, is more than survival. To live, to most people, means the same thing. They want to be healthy, happy, reasonably prosperous, secure, and have friends, peace of mind, good family relationships, and hope.

But just like the caterpillar, many people just go around and around, following along behind another person—with life only six inches away. Many young people go to class today because they went yesterday. They go to practice because they have to if they want to play. They wear the clothes, listen to the music, and do the things they do because they are just following the other caterpillars. They grow up and take jobs and go to work each day because they went the day before. They look forward to retirement because they don't like what they do.

Instead of being a caterpillar and simply following and never enjoying life, be responsible to live—to get every minute out of every day. Do that today. Instead of just going to English class, go with a purpose. Learn something in every class you go to today. Get up 30 minutes earlier. Remember, you are eventually going to be "asleep" a lot longer than you will be alive. Get up and enjoy 30 more minutes of tomorrow than you did today.

Go to practice today with a passion to get something done. Refuse to be a caterpillar. Be a butterfly. Break out of the cocoon and eat the pine needles. Enjoy life. Make a commitment to get something positive out of everything you do.

Do: (15 minutes)

- Lead the team through a discussion on the questions found on the student worksheet. Be sure to get specific examples.
- Review the word of the day. Ask a student to use it correctly in a sentence.

Photo Credit: Darren England/Getty Images Sport

LESSON #9

LIVING A BUTTERFLY LIFE—WORKSHEET

"If you want to hit a bird on the wing you must have all your will in focus, you must be thinking about yourself and, equally, you must not be thinking about your neighbor: you must be living in your eye on that bird. Every achievement is a bird on the wing."

—Oliver Wendell Holmes Jr.

For discussion:

1. Give examples of the caterpillar mentality.

_____

_____

_____

_____

2. List steps to avoid the caterpillar mentality.

_____

_____

_____

_____

3. Write down one thing you are going to accomplish in practice today.

_____

_____

_____

_____

Word of the Day: Focus—a center of interest or activity

A LESSON IN ACCOUNTABILITY—COACH'S NOTES

LESSON #10

Say: (5 minutes)

According to the dictionary definition, being responsible means you are answerable, expected to account for something, dependable or reliable, as in meeting an obligation.

What can being responsible do for you? In a study of men who had started with nothing and became millionaires, the one thing that was unique was that they had all been given responsibilities at a very early age. They had jobs. Some of the jobs were small, but the men learned the responsibility of taking care of small jobs. If you learn responsibility, you are on the road to successful living.

Learning is gaining knowledge. Living is using that knowledge to improve yourself. You have learned responsibility. Now it is time to put it to work.

Behavioral scientists say that it takes 21 consecutive days of doing something to form a habit. You are going to begin forming habits of responsibility today. Pick one thing that you are going to be responsible for, write it down, sign it, and have your "accountability partner" sign it also. Your partner is then going to make sure you don't drop the ball. He will be positive and encouraging, but he is going to hold you accountable.

Consider the following affirmations:
* I will make my bed every day for 21 days.
* I will wash the dishes for my mom every day for 21 days.
* I will read a positive book for one hour each day for 21 days.
* I will get up 30 minutes earlier every day for 21 days.

Write down your task. The group will be checking on you. You know responsibility, now you must exhibit it.

Do: (15 minutes)

* Have each student individually fill out the "Contract for Success" found on the student worksheet.
* Have each team member pick someone else on the team to become his partner.
* Have the partners sign each other's contracts.
* Ask volunteers to share what they have written down as what they are going to do.
* Review the word of the day. Ask a student to use it correctly in a sentence.

LESSON #10

A LESSON IN ACCOUNTABILITY—WORKSHEET

"If you wish your merit to be known, acknowledge that of other people."
—Chinese Proverb

My Contract for Success:

I plan to show responsibility in the following areas:

_____

_____

_____

_____

I will be responsible for these things by taking the following action steps:

_____

_____

_____

_____

Today, _____, I, _____, am making
a commitment to myself to start my plan by taking the following first step:

_____

_____

Signed: _____

Signed: _____
accountability partner

Word of the Day: Merit—high level of superiority; worth

PLAYING TIME—COACH'S NOTES

Say: (5 minutes)

All athletics are "pay to play." When you begin sports at a young age, the rules are very strict. Because your parents pay a certain amount of money, you are guaranteed a certain number of innings, minutes, or quarters. It is your parents' responsibility to pay so that you might play. This idea is sometimes ingrained within the parent—that because you are on the team, you should get to play. It is easy to see how they form that opinion. From the time you participate in your first athletic contest, it is understood that everyone will get to play. It is the shared responsibility of the parents to pay and the coach to get you into the game for the proper amount of time. If this doesn't happen, serious consequences occur. If everyone doesn't play, the team may have to forfeit and the coach may not be allowed to coach anymore. This idea has caught on and continues many times all the way through junior high athletics and even in some cases to the junior varsity level.

Coaches at these levels usually have players for only one year. The seventh grade coach usually only coaches seventh grade, so to keep peace, because of a belief that participation and not winning is the objective, he usually makes every effort to play every player. The responsibility for playing time remains mostly with the coach

Every coach at a sub-varsity level has had a parent explain that winning and losing at that level is unimportant. That is, if "Johnny" comes to practice, he should get to play. Many coaches say many similar things: "Let them all play."

The only problem with this is determining when the will to win becomes important to the players. Most coaches would probably agree with Bobby Knight, who said that the most important attribute is the will to prepare to win. You cannot believe both. If, because you come to practice, you deserve to play until your varsity years, that means you will spend perhaps 10 years learning one way of thinking and then have to change it in one or two years, as will your parents.

You, the players, are responsible for your playing time. Pay to play is still in effect. The only difference is you are now the one paying. If you pay, you get to play. I think every player should be told what the price is to play. (*Note*: Use your own sports example here.) For example, if you are a lineman, you must have the following specific skills to play:
*   Know all your assignments. Know who to block on every play.
*   Physically, you must be able to prevent defenders from causing damage to the teammate with the football.

The list is very short and very easily evaluated. If a person playing on the offensive line cannot do these two things, he should not be allowed to play in a game. When he becomes proficient at these two things, he then has a chance to play.

The coach's responsibility is simple. Tell the player what it is that he must do to be able to play. It is then up to the player to meet these criteria. The player, once the cost is understood, has to pay before playing.

It is also important that you understand that it is not your teammates' responsibility to see that you play. How many times have you heard, "We were ahead/behind by 20 points. He should have allowed you to play." This statement means that your playing time is dictated by your teammates. They either have to be good enough to win by large margins or bad enough to lose by large margins before you are capable of playing. In other words, your playing time is totally in someone else's hands. Regardless of the score, every one of you wants to have the responsibility to determine whether or not you play. That is why each coach gives you the criteria it will take for you to start and to play. These two lists are different, but they are both specific and evaluative. *You*, not your parents, nor your teammates, then become responsible for if and when you play.

Athletics will teach you to be responsible if you will accept the responsibility. Give the list to your parents and explain your weaknesses. They want to help but they are not responsible. *You are.*

Do: (15 minutes)

- Discuss the questions found on the student worksheet.
- Review the word of the day. Ask a student to use it correctly in a sentence.

PLAYING TIME—WORKSHEET

"For the want of a nail, the shoe was lost, for the want of a shoe the horse was lost; and for the want of a horse the rider was lost, being overtaken and slain by the enemy, all for the want of care about a horseshoe nail.

—Benjamin Franklin

For discussion:

1. What must you do to be a starter?

_____

_____

_____

_____

2. What must you do to play?

_____

_____

_____

_____

3. What is the difference in "pay to play" between Little League and interscholastic sports?

_____

_____

_____

_____

Word of the Day: Preparation—process of getting ready for some purpose, task, or event

STRUGGLES—COACH'S NOTES

Say: (5 minutes)

When he was a small boy, he had loved butterflies. Not to net and mount them, but to wonder at their designs and habits. Now a grown man with his first son to be born in a few weeks, he found himself once again fascinated with a cocoon. He had found it at the side of the park path. Somehow the fragile case had been knocked from the tree and the cocoon had survived undamaged and still woven to the branch.

As he had seen his mother do, he gently protected it by wrapping it in his handkerchief and carrying it home. The cocoon found a temporary home in a wide-top mason jar with holes in the lid. The jar was placed on the mantel for easy viewing and protected from their curious cat, who would delight in volleying the sticky silk between his paws.

The man watched his wife's interest, which lasted only a moment, but he studied the silky envelope. Almost imperceptibly at first, the cocoon moved. He watched more closely and soon the cocoon was trembling with activity. Nothing else happened. The cocoon remained tightly glued to the twig and no sign of wings existed.

Finally, the shaking became so intense that the man thought the butterfly would die from the struggle. He removed the lid on the jar, took a sharp penknife from his desk drawer, and carefully made a tiny slit in the side of the cocoon. Almost immediately, one wing appeared and then out stretched the other. The butterfly was free. It seemed to enjoy its freedom and walked along the edge of the mantel. But it did not fly. At first the man thought the wings needed time to dry, but time passed and still the butterfly did not take off.

The man was worried and called his neighbor, who taught high school science. He told the neighbor how he found the cocoon, placed it in the mason jar, and the terrible trembling as the butterfly struggled to get out. When he discovered how the man had carefully made a small slit in the cocoon, the teacher stopped him, "Oh, that is the reason. You see, the struggle is what gives the butterfly the strength to fly." And so it is with people. Sometimes it is the struggles in life that strengthen you the most and give you the ability to fly.

People complain most often about adversity, about the struggles they face. You should be thankful for those struggles. It is the adversity and struggles that make character rise to the top. Every experience you have will make you stronger. Learn to see adversity and struggle as opportunities to grow.

Do: (15 minutes)

- Lead a discussion from the questions on the student worksheet. Be sure to let the students do the talking and always ask for specific examples.
- Review the word of the day. Ask a student to use it correctly in a sentence.

STRUGGLES—WORKSHEET

"That which does not kill me, makes me stronger."

—Friedrich Nietzsche

For discussion:

1. What struggles have you had that helped you become a better person?

_____

_____

_____

2. Do you know of a classmate who is shielded from struggling? What affect do you see in their personality?

_____

_____

_____

3. How can you condition yourself to look at struggles in a positive light?

_____

_____

_____

4. What lesson can you take from this story and apply to something that is happening today?

_____

_____

_____

Word of the Day: Struggle—to make strenuous efforts against opposition

LESSON #13

LOVING: WILLING TO GIVE UP SELF FOR OTHERS OR SOMEONE ELSE—COACH'S NOTES

Say: (5 minutes)

Love is the greatest motivating factor in the world. However, the opposite of love is not hate. The opposite of love is selfishness.

Consider the following story: During the evacuation of Saigon in the last days of the Vietnam War, a little Vietnamese girl's 12-year-old brother brought her into an army medical unit. The little girl was in serious need of a blood transfusion. Without it she would probably die. The doctor spoke no Vietnamese and the boy spoke no English. The doctor finally got across to the young boy that he needed him as a blood donor so that the girl could live. He laid the boy on a gurney beside his sister and started the transfusion. Later he returned, and the little girl seemed to be feeling better, but the boy was crying quietly and appeared to be in pain. They found an interpreter and asked the boy what was wrong. He responded, "When do I die?" The boy was unclear about the procedure and thought he had to give all of his blood to his sister. He was willing to give up his life for the life of his sister.

When someone asked Bill Curry, an offensive lineman with the Green Bay Packers, what it was that made the Packers such a great team during the 1960s, he replied: "When it's the fourth quarter, when it's 99 degrees, 100 percent humidity, and your legs feel like anvils—the right one won't go in front of the left—you're behind by four points with 35 yards to go, and you know you've got to score, the main thing that makes me come back up to the ball is the fact that the guys next to me feel the same way I do. And I know, because I've seen them do it time and again, that they are going to come off the ball a little bit harder than they did the time before. Somehow, with this reserve of strength or courage or moral fiber or commitment to each other or love or concern or whatever you want to call it—which means I've got to do it if I want to be a part of this. So I will come back off the ball, and I'll hit the guy in front of me and his numbers with all my might again and again. It's so I can go back in the locker room, after having gained those last 35 yards and won the game, and walk back in there with my arm around my teammate, and know that we did that together. We gave it a little more than we really had. Now that may sound real phony, but I promise you it's the reason we play."

Do: (15 minutes)

- Lead a discussion from the questions on the student worksheet. Be sure to let the students do the talking and always ask for specific examples.
- Review the word of the day. Ask a student to use it correctly in a sentence.

LOVING: WILLING TO GIVE UP SELF FOR OTHERS OR SOMEONE ELSE—WORKSHEET

"I believe that one can conquer fear by doing the things he fears to do, provided he keeps doing them until he gets a record of successful experiences behind him."

—Eleanor Roosevelt

For discussion:

1. What story emphasizes love to you? Why?

_____

_____

_____

_____

2. Who is the most loving person you know? Why?

_____

_____

_____

_____

3. Why would selfishness be the opposite of love?

_____

_____

_____

_____

Word of the Day: Selfish—concerned excessively or exclusively with oneself; seeking or concentrating on one's own advantage, pleasure, or well-being without regard for others

RESPONSE TO DISCIPLINE—COACH'S NOTES

Say: (5 minutes)

One out of 100 people at the age of 65 is financially independent. That one person needs no assistance from the government or from his relatives to have a quality lifestyle.

The number one employer of people over age 65 is Wal-Mart*. The second is McDonald's*. It is unlikely that anyone sets their life's goal to either be dependent upon others or to be working at Wal-Mart or McDonald's when they are 65 years old.

In athletics, many cry at the end of the season because they did not reach their goals, or they cry in the off-season because of the pain they're experiencing, either through intense physical workouts or because of all the leisure-time activities they are foregoing to achieve their goal.

Academics are the same. When people walk in to be tested, they will experience either "pain of discipline" or "pain of regret." If they have disciplined themselves to study and prepare, they are excited about the opportunity to be tested. If not, they have the experience of regret.

Every individual is experiencing two ages simultaneously—a chronological age and a mental age. The chronological age is the number of years he has been alive. The mental age is determined, according to at least one psychologist, by the ability to sacrifice a short-term pleasure for a long-range goal. It is possible to have some 14-year-old "adults" and some 40-year-old "children."

Do: (15 minutes)

- Lead a discussion from the questions on the student worksheet. Be sure to let the students do the talking and always ask for specific examples.
- Review the word of the day. Ask a student to use it correctly in a sentence.

RESPONSE TO DISCIPLINE—WORKSHEET

"He who gains victory over other men is strong; but he who gains victory over himself is all powerful."

—Lao-Tzu

For discussion:

1. What is a short-term pleasure? A long-range goal?

_____

_____

_____

_____

_____

2. Give an example in your life of the pain of discipline and of the pain of regret.

_____

_____

_____

_____

_____

3. What will it take to make your mental age higher than your chronological age?

_____

_____

_____

_____

Word of the Day: Goal—the end toward which effort is directed

LESSON #15

KNOWLEDGE—COACH'S NOTES

Say: (5 minutes)

Knowledge is defined as the body of truth, information, and principles acquired by mankind.

Consider the following story: One year at a high school all-star football game, a former NFL player came in and talked to the players. He told them he knew that every player there had high expectations and dreams of playing professional football. He also explained how athletics had been his very best friend and had given him self-worth and a positive self-image. Because of his friend, athletics, he was the big man on campus. He dated the prettiest girls and was invited to the best parties. After college, the player was drafted and athletics, his best friend, made him rich and famous.

Then one day, his best friend deserted him. His coach called him in and said he could no longer play football. His friend, athletics, was absolutely nowhere to be found; it had abandoned him. If his college coach had not forced him to go to class and get a degree, he would have been left out in the cold. He found out his best friend was really academics, especially his degree, because no one could take that away from him. The knowledge he had acquired and the degree he had earned were truly his best friends. Today, he is a successful businessman, not because of athletics, but because of his good friend, academics.

Athletics may receive the spotlight, but academics endure. Athletic ability will eventually deteriorate. Academics and knowledge never will. Athletics and extracurricular activities are available at public schools to enhance academics. Unfortunately, some schools and students have put these activities ahead of academics. People who only value athletics/extracurricular activities pay a terrible price later. Knowledge is a student's true friend, and knowledge comes from academics, not athletics.

Do: (15 minutes)

- Lead a discussion from the questions on the student worksheet. Be sure to let the students do the talking and always ask for specific examples.
- Review the word of the day. Ask a student to use it correctly in a sentence.

KNOWLEDGE—WORKSHEET

"All men by nature desire knowledge."

—Aristotle

For discussion:

1. Why does society view knowledge as being less desirable than fame?

    _____

    _____

    _____

2. Which is your best friend—athletics, extracurricular activities, or academics? Why?

    _____

    _____

    _____

3. If academics/knowledge is your best friend, how should you treat it?

    _____

    _____

    _____

4. Do you treat it this way? Why or why not?

    _____

    _____

    _____

Word of the Day: Friend—one attached to another by affection or esteem; a favored companion

SELF-IMAGE

"A man wrapped up in himself makes a very small bundle."

—Benjamin Franklin

Chapter 4

IMPORTANCE OF SELF-IMAGE (PART 1)— COACH'S NOTES

SAY: (5 MINUTES)

During a break in a prison ministry presentation, Bill Glass asked Jim Sundberg how it was that he came to be an outstanding Major League Baseball catcher. Sundberg replied that his dad was always telling him that he would end up being a Major League catcher. Sundberg said that he didn't want to disappoint his dad. A prison inmate was standing nearby and quietly said, "I didn't disappoint my dad, either." Bill Glass asked him what he meant. "You see," the inmate continued, "from the time I was a child my dad always told me I would end up in prison, and sure enough, here I am."

Two different stories. The opposite ends of the spectrum. This story shows the picture that two men were given of themselves. Self-image is very simply the picture each person has of himself. This picture or portrait has been painted by everything you experience. Everything that has been said or done to you has made this portrait what it is. How important is this concept of self-image?

Consider the following quote from leading psychologist, Dr. Joyce Brothers: "An individual's self-concept (image) is the core of his personality. It affects every aspect of human behavior: the ability to learn, the capacity to grow and change, the choice of friends, mates, and careers. It's no exaggeration to say that a strong, positive self-image is the best possible preparation for success in life."

Examine the following statement closely, piece by piece:

> *"It affects every aspect of human behavior: the ability to learn..."*

A person with a poor picture of himself does not believe he can learn, and his report card bears this out. When Victor Seribriakoff was 15, his teacher told him that he would never finish school and that he should drop out and learn a trade. Victor took the advice and for the next 17 years he was an itinerant doing a variety of odd jobs. He had been told he was a "dunce," and for 17 years he acted like one. When he was 32 years old, an amazing transformation took place. In the course of applying for a job, he took an IQ test. The evaluation revealed that he was a genius with an IQ of 161. Guess what happened then? He started acting like a genius. Since that time, he has written books, secured a number of patents, and become a successful businessman.

From the time the teacher told him that he was a dunce until he took the IQ test, did he acquire a tremendous amount of additional knowledge? No. What changed was the picture. He went from having a picture of himself as a dunce to seeing himself as a genius. When he saw himself as a dunce, he acted like a dunce. When he saw himself as a genius, he acted like a genius. What is the picture you have of yourself with regard to learning?

> *"...the capacity to grow and change..."*

Linda Isaacs' family, friends, and teachers saw her as a dwarf of limited mental capabilities, so that's the way they treated her. Her teachers in the special education classes in Italy, Texas, didn't think she could learn, so they didn't attempt to teach her much. They passed her from one grade to the next until she "graduated" from high school. L:inda was then a four-foot-tall, 80-pound, black high school graduate who functioned at the first-grade level. Under these circumstances, Linda had two chances in life—slim and none. Then her mother contacted Carol Clapp at the Texas Rehabilitation Commission at Goodwill Industries. As a result, Linda moved to Dallas to live with a sister and started an extensive three-week vocational program. She was placed in a work adjustment program where a different crop was planted in her mind. She quickly outgrew that program and was transferred to the Industrial Contract Center.

She now takes telephone messages, keeps time cards, and checks each day's progress. Her personality changed as her confidence grew under this "new" treatment. She joined the Little People of America and wants to be a secretary; she loves life, likes what she is doing, and her image is such that she no longer minds being call "Shorty." Linda Isaacs' story is one that will probably have a happy ending, but it does make you wonder how many people have been consigned to mediocrity by someone who saw them in an inferior light and treated them accordingly.

Where was Linda Isaacs' growth and change? Why? When her picture changed, she grew.

> "...the choice of friends, mates, and careers..."

If you have a low picture of yourself, who would you choose as your friends? What if you have a good picture of yourself? By the same token, who would you choose as your mate if you have a low picture of yourself? What if you have a good picture of yourself?

Career? What are some possible choices a person with a low self-image would make? How about someone with good self-image?

> "...strong positive self-image is the best possible preparation for success in life."

The job of a coach is to give you the best preparation for success in life. In the next 20 lessons, you are going to understand that you...

> "...were designed for accomplishment, engineered for success, and endowed with the seeds of greatness."
>
> —Zig Ziglar

DO: (15 MINUTES)

- Lead a discussion covering the questions found on the student worksheet.
- Review the word of the day. Ask a student to use it correctly in a sentence.

LESSON #1

IMPORTANCE OF SELF-IMAGE (PART 1)— WORKSHEET

"Without self-knowledge, without understanding the working and function of his machine, man cannot be free, he cannot govern himself and he will always remain a slave."

—George Gurdjieff

For discussion:

1. What is the picture you have of yourself with regard to learning? Of what importance to you is the Victor Seribriakoff story?

   _____

   _____

2. What made Linda Isaacs able to learn new skills after going through 12 years of school, learning very little?

   _____

   _____

3. What do you need to make you grow?

   _____

   _____

4. How do you choose your friends?

   _____

   _____

5. What careers are you thinking of pursuing?

   _____

   _____

Word of the Day: Introspection—examination of one's thoughts and feelings

IMPORTANCE OF SELF-IMAGE (PART 2)—
COACH'S NOTES

SAY: (5 MINUTES)

Maxwell Maltz, M.D., FICS, was one of the world's most widely known and highly regarded plastic surgeons. He found that a plastic surgeon does not simply alter a man's face. He alters the man's inner self. Maltz wrote of the amazing changes that often occur quite suddenly and dramatically in a person's personality when you change his face. But he learned more from his failures than from his successes. Some patients showed no change in personality after surgery and continued to feel inferior or inadequate. It was as if the personality itself had a "face." The nonphysical "face of personality" seemed to be the real key to personality change. If it remained "ugly" or inferior, the person himself acted out this role in his behavior, regardless of the changes in physical appearance. Maltz discovered that the "inner picture," not the "outer picture," was the real key to personality and behavior.

If it were the outer picture that is important, then a boy who is teased for having big ears and then has those ears corrected and the object of his humiliation removed, would then assume a normal role in life. From this event, you could theorize that the "cure all" for all inferiority, unhappiness, and failures would be wholesale plastic surgery. However, following this logic, people with "normal faces" (outer picture) should be completely free from all psychological handicaps, which everyone knows is simply not true. What Maltz discovered was that the determining factor in all cases was the person's self-image. This image sets the parameters of what the person thinks he can or cannot do.

You must have a self-image that is both adequate and realistic. You must be acceptable to you. You must have a self that you are not ashamed to be. You must know your strengths and your weaknesses and be honest with yourself concerning both. Your self-image must be a reasonable approximation of "you"—neither more than you are nor less than you are.

The bottom line that you can learn from the plastic surgeon is that it is not what is on the outside that determines your success. It is your inner picture, the self-image that sets the parameters or limits of your success.

DO: (15 MINUTES)

- Give the students 10 minutes to complete all three questions.
- Ask for volunteers to share answers from Question #2.
- Review the word of the day. Ask a student to use it correctly in a sentence.

LESSON #2

LESSON #2: IMPORTANCE OF SELF-IMAGE (PART 2)—WORKSHEET

"Fortunate, indeed, is the man who takes exactly the right measure of himself, and holds a just balance between what he can acquire and what he can use."

—Peter Mere Latham

For discussion:

1. A healthy self-image is balanced. You must know and use your strengths as well as be aware of, and work on, your weaknesses. List your strengths and weaknesses. (Be honest with yourself. This is for you.) Use the list below to help you begin.

• Honest	• Decisive	• Indecisive
• Confident	• Fast learner	• Disorganized
• Patient	• Dependable	• Slow learner
• Loving	• Organized	• Impatient
• Friendly	• Integrity	• Bad work ethic
• Disciplined	• Loyal	• Undisciplined
• Persistent	• Compassionate	• Antisocial
• Knowledgeable	• Strong character	
• Dedicated	• Strong work ethic	

    Remember, you are concerned with the inner-self, not the outer-self.

    My Strengths   My Weaknesses

    _____   _____

    _____   _____

    _____   _____

2. Your "inner picture" is formed by the experiences you have had. Write of an experience you have had that caused you to feel good about yourself.

    _____

    _____

3. Almost everyone also has an ideal "image"; the person you want to be. List these characteristics, using the list above to trigger your thoughts.

    _____

    _____

Word of the Day: Balance—stability between opposing forces

IDENTIFYING A POOR SELF-IMAGE—COACH'S NOTES

LESSON #3

SAY: (10 MINUTES)

It is easy to spot people who don't feel good about themselves, who have a poor picture of themselves. Tell-tale signs can help you identify a poor self-image. The first step to correcting a problem is to recognize that you have a problem. The alcoholic must first admit that he is dependent upon alcohol before anything can be done about the addiction. Recognizing the signs of a weak picture provides a chance to repair that picture. You may have once blamed others for your faults, but you now know that you are responsible for your picture, no matter how it came to be.

At least 95 percent of people have their lives lessened by feelings of inferiority to some extent, and to these millions, this same feeling of inferiority is a serious handicap to success and happiness. In one sense of the word, every person on the face of the earth is inferior to some other person or persons. You know that you cannot lift as much weight as Bill Pearl, throw a football like Peyton Manning, or dance like Cyd Charisse. This knowledge should not induce feelings of inferiority and lessen your quality of life. Nor should it make you feel that you are no good merely because you cannot do certain things as skillfully or as well as they can. Remember, every person you meet is inferior to you in certain respects. You can do certain things better than your best friend, but that fact should not make you feel superior any more than a comparison to Troy Aikman should make you feel inferior.

Feelings of inferiority originate not so much from facts or experience, but from your conclusions regarding facts, and your evaluation of experiences. For example, being inferior to the great Bill Pearl in weightlifting does not make you inferior to Bill Pearl.

It is not knowledge of actual inferiority or lack of skill or knowledge that gives you a bad picture; it is the *feeling* of inferiority that does this. And this feeling—this inferior picture—comes about for just one reason: You judge yourself, and measure yourself, not against your own norm or standard but against some other individual's norm. When you do this, you always, without exception, come out second best. But because you trust and believe and assume that you should measure up to some other person's picture, you feel miserable and second-rate and conclude that something is wrong with you. The next logical conclusion in this confused reasoning process is that you are not worthy, that you do not deserve success or happiness, and that it would inappropriate for you to fully express your abilities and talents, whatever they might be, without apology or without feeling guilty about it.

All of these feelings come about because you have bought into the erroneous idea that "I should be like so-and-so" or "I should be like everyone else." The major fallacy of "everybody else" is that "everybody else" is composed of individuals, no two of whom are alike.

A person with an inferior picture invariably compounds the error by striving for superiority. His feelings spring from the false premise that he is inferior. From this false premise he decides that the cure—the way to feel good—is to make himself superior.

This striving for superiority gets him into more trouble and causes more frustration. He becomes more miserable than ever, and the harder he tries, the more miserable he becomes.

The cure is simple—the truth about you is this: You are not inferior. You are not superior. You are simply *you*.

You as a personality are not in competition with any other personality, simply because no other person on earth is like you. You are unique. You are not supposed to be like any other person and nobody is supposed to be like you.

No "standard person" exists. Like snowflakes, every person is individual and unique. Short, tall, large, small, black, yellow, red, or white—no perfect individual exists. Abraham Lincoln once said, "God must have loved the common people, for he made so many of them." He was wrong. There is no "common man." He would have been nearer the truth had he said, "God must have loved the uncommon people for he made so many of them."

An inferior picture and its accompanying deterioration in performance can be made to order in the psychological laboratory. All you need to do is set up a "standard" picture, and then convince your subject that he does not measure up. A psychologist wanted to test this concept. He gave his students a set of routine tests. Then, he solemnly announced that the average person could complete the test in about one-fifth the time it would really take. When, in the course of the test a bell would ring, indicating that the "average man's time" was up, some of the brightest subjects became very jittery and incompetent, indeed thinking themselves to be morons.

Stop measuring yourself against someone else's standard. You are not "them" and can never measure up. Neither can "they" measure up to your standards, nor should they. Once you see this simple, self-evident truth, accept it and believe it, your inferior feelings will vanish.

DO: (10 MINUTES)

- Lead a discussion covering the questions found on the student worksheet.
- Review the word of the day. Ask a student to use it correctly in a sentence.

IDENTIFYING A POOR SELF-IMAGE—WORKSHEET

LESSON #3

"No one can make you feel inferior without your permission."

—Eleanor Roosevelt

For discussion:

1. Whose standard have you been trying to live up to?

_____

_____

_____

_____

2. Write down some of your "unique" qualities.

_____

_____

_____

_____

3. What do you think Eleanor Roosevelt meant when she said, "No one can make you feel inferior without your permission"?

_____

_____

_____

_____

_____

Word of the Day: Expectation—eager anticipation of something coming

CAUSES OF POOR SELF-IMAGE—COACH'S NOTES

SAY: (5 MINUTES)

If self-image is so important, why is it that so many people have a poor self-image? The number one reason is the impact of a largely negative society.

When a baby elephant is born into a circus, the trainers take a one-inch steel band and weld it onto the young elephant's leg. It is then connected with a heavy-duty chain to a post concreted into the ground. The baby is given enough chain to go only as far as the trainers will allow. The baby elephant knows no boundaries and takes off to explore the world. When it reaches the end of the chain it is immediately jerked off its feet. Undaunted, it takes off again, only to end up with the same results. When you go to a circus you will find one of the largest and strongest animals on earth secured only by a rope wrapped around a stake driven into the ground. The elephant can go until the rope tightens and then it stops. It is mentally within the parameters of where it can go.

Young people begin with great dreams and aspirations. You will never meet a child who aspires to be a drug addict, school dropout, or failure. They begin by wanting to be president or have other ambitious aspirations. They get knocked down by the negative society around them until the picture they have of themselves is just as binding mentally as the rope on the elephant's foot.

Every person begins life untethered. As you have experiences and grow, negative people start putting chains on your feet. Negative society tries to set parameters for your success. An endless group of people will tell you what you cannot do. The negative society gives "opinions" of why you can't be successful. The fact is, at one time or another, someone has overcome that "opinion" and become successful.

Remember what Eleanor Roosevelt once said: "No one can make you feel inferior without your permission." If you have a poor self-image because of the negative people you have been around, it is because you have given them permission to affect you. Rescind that permission and start changing that picture today.

DO: (15 MINUTES)

- Lead the team through a discussion covering the questions found on the student worksheet.
- Review the word of the day. Ask a student to use it correctly in a sentence.

CAUSES OF POOR SELF-IMAGE—WORKSHEET

"Many persons have the wrong idea of what constitutes true happiness. It is not attained through self-gratification, but through fidelity to a worthy purpose."

—Helen Keller

For discussion:

1. Identify ways people try to set boundaries for your success.

    _____

    _____

    _____

    _____

2. For each way identified in Question #1, develop a plan to overcome it.

    _____

    _____

    _____

    _____

3. List at least three sources of negative input you have in your life. List at least three positive sources of input you have in your life. What can you do to minimize the negative input and maximize the positive input?

    _____

    _____

    _____

    _____

    _____

Word of the Day: Fidelity—loyalty; faithfulness

ACCENTUATE THE POSITIVE, ELIMINATE THE NEGATIVE—COACH'S NOTES

SAY: (5 MINUTES)

Gentleman Jim Corbett, the former heavyweight boxing champion, was out running one morning when he noticed a man fishing. He stopped and watched. The man would catch a large fish and throw it back. The only fish he kept were the smaller ones. Thinking this odd, he asked the fisherman why he kept the small ones and threw back the big ones. "I only have a small frying pan," was the reply.

You may think this fisherman is not very bright, but many similar "fishermen" are in this room and in rooms throughout this country. People don't get the best things in life because someone has convinced them that they only have a "small frying pan." Many don't expect or even want the great things because someone or something has "conditioned" them into believing that they do not deserve them.

It is no exaggeration to say that every human being is conditioned to some extent, either by ideas he has uncritically accepted from others or ideas he has repeated to himself or convinced himself are true. These negative ideas have a serious impact on a person's behavior and performance.

The basic problem is that too many young people have no idea what they can do because all they've ever been told is what they can't do. They have no idea what they want because they have no idea what's available *for them*. It's easy for them to understand how others can do wonderful things and win big games, but they can't see the same things for themselves. They suffer from PLOM (Poor Little Ol' Me) disease.

You must change the picture you have of yourself. How?

- Remember that failure is an event, not a person. Yesterday really did end last night. Today is a brand new day, and it's yours to start on a winning streak.
- Understand that the opinion you have of yourself is the most important opinion you have. The most important conversation you have is the conversation you have with yourself.
- Remember, you were born to win. But to be a winner, you must plan to win and prepare to win, and only then can you legitimately expect to win.
- Understand that the input your mind receives determines your outlook on life. Your outlook determines your output, and your output determines the outcomes of your life. You have to diligently search for the kind of input that will help you change the picture.
- Think of 10 positive things that others have said about you or you believe about yourself. Examples may include enthusiastic, disciplined, honest, friendly, cheerful, positive, hard-working, team player, dependable, or optimistic. Every night just before bedtime and every morning just before you leave for school, remember these qualities, get in front of a mirror, look yourself in the eye and say, "I, _____, am an enthusiastic, disciplined, honest, friendly,

cheerful, positive, hard-working, dependable, and optimistic team-player. These qualities are the ones I was born to embody." Do this process for 30 days and you will undoubtedly like yourself better and perform better.

Fortunately, this change of input will affect every area of your life. Personal performance on the field will improve, as will your performance in the classroom.

Dr. Alfred Adler was told as a young man that he was not good in mathematics. His parents were told the same thing and for years he went along with this picture in his mind. One day, sitting in math class, he thought he knew how to solve a very difficult problem. His teacher and classmates laughed at the idea of Alfred Adler solving the problem. With total indignation, he went to the chalkboard and solved the problem. He refused to allow someone to paint him as incapable. It was not until he was ridiculed and the humiliation caused him to rise up that he changed his "picture." What humiliation would it take for you to change your "picture"?

The message is clear. To achieve your maximum, you have to "recondition" yourself from the negative beliefs that may have been painted in you. The first and most important thing is that you must understand that the way you have been living and what you have been dreaming are based on beliefs that you have been conditioned to accept as true.

It is now time for you to take a personal inventory. As you do this inventory, recognize the changes the positive conditioning has made—or is in the process of making—to your beliefs.

DO: (15 MINUTES)

- Allow 10 minutes for the team to individually fill out the worksheet.
- Briefly lead a discussion on the questions at the bottom of the student worksheet.
- Review the word of the day. Ask a student to use it correctly in a sentence.

LESSON #5

ACCENTUATE THE POSITIVE, ELIMINATE THE NEGATIVE—WORKSHEET

"To know what you prefer, instead of humbly saying 'Amen' to what the world tells you you ought to prefer, is to keep your soul alive."

—Robert Louis Stevenson

Confidential:

Write down beliefs you have about yourself in the following areas:

• Intelligence (How smart are you?) _____

• Ability to learn math _____

• Maturity (willing to sacrifice a short-term pleasure for a long-range goal)
_____

• Responsibility (accountable for something or someone)_____

_____

• Honesty (integrity) _____

• Work ethic (hard worker or lazy) _____

• Future (What do you expect in one year, five years, 10 years, and 20 years?)_____

_____

For discussion:

1. Look back at this personal inventory. How big is your frying pan?

    _____

    _____

2. What did you learn from today?

    _____

    _____

Word of the Day: Propriety—conformity to accepted standards of social conduct

FAILURE IS AN EVENT, NOT A PERSON— COACH'S NOTES

LESSON #6

SAY: (5 MINUTES)

A major cause of poor self-image is that people often confuse failing in an event with being a failure as a person. Every person fails at something. Michael Jordan is perhaps the greatest basketball player who has ever played the game. He retired from basketball and made an effort to play Major League Baseball. He never made it to the "Big Leagues." Do you think Michael Jordan is a failure? No one would ever consider him a failure. He failed to make the grade in baseball. That event did not make him a failure.

In baseball, Reggie Jackson became known as "Mr. October" because of his heroics in the playoffs and World Series. He was eventually inducted into the Baseball Hall of Fame. Reggie Jackson was also a failure at baseball! He struck out more than anyone who has ever played baseball. What kind of self-images do you think Reggie Jackson and Michael Jordan have? They have distinguished failing in an event from *being* a failure. Failure is a verb that describes on action; it means the inability to reach an objective. Failure is not a person.

Many people misdefine failure because as youngsters their ability, appearance, and intelligence have been ridiculed or questioned repeatedly by parents, teachers, friends, and others in authority. In many cases, these injuries come in the form of insinuation and innuendo, but they are just as real and devastating as if they were true. Many times, even a chance or unintentional remark starts the negative slide that is then fed by hurts that are real or imagined. The net result is that a person sees himself through the negative eyes of others. If your friends, family, and associates find constant fault with you, you will get a distorted picture of the real you.

Exaggeration by parents and friends often begins painting a picture that becomes all too real. "You are the clumsiest boy in the world." "You forget everything." "You are always breaking things." The destructiveness of this approach should be obvious but, unfortunately, it is often anything but obvious. The classroom put-downs imply that a person is a failure rather than that a person has failed to do something.

Combine the tendency to insult with some phase of physical appearance (e.g., obesity, bad teeth, poor complexion, crooked smile, bad eyesight, too tall, too short) and you have all the ingredients for the beginning of a bad self-image. The child then reasons that since he or she is "ugly," "dumb," or "inept," he doesn't deserve the good things in life and has no chance for success. This point is critically important, because survey after survey shows that 95 percent of American youth would change their appearance if they could.

The aforementioned list of failures of Abraham Lincoln (In Chapter 2) provides an excellent example of the fact that failure does not define the person. To paraphrase Wendell Phillips on the subject, "failure is nothing but education; nothing but the first step to something better."

DO: (15 MINUTES)

- Divide the team into smaller work groups.
- Assign Questions #1–3 to one or more groups, assign Questions #4–5 to one or more groups, and assign Question #6 to one or more groups.
- Have group leaders report back on their answers.
- Review the word of the day. Ask a student to use it correctly in a sentence.

Photo Credit: Scott Halleran/Getty Images Sport

FAILURE IS AN EVENT, NOT A PERSON— WORKSHEET

"The successful person is the individual who forms the habit of doing what the failing person doesn't like to do."

—Donald Riggs

For discussion:

1. Did Abraham Lincoln fail? Was he a failure?

_____

_____

2. Why do you think his self-image was not affected by the failures?

_____

_____

3. What can you learn from Lincoln's experiences?

_____

_____

4. List "put-downs" you hear daily that affect others or your own self-image.

_____

_____

5. Why do people not recognize the devastation their comments cause?

_____

_____

6. What is the difference between failing and being a failure?

_____

_____

Word of the Day: Success—achievement of something desired, intended, or attempted

YOU ARE A THIEF—COACH'S NOTES

SAY: (5 MINUTES)

The most puzzling and disappointing incident in the sports world occurs in baseball when a batter steps up to the plate and proceeds to let the pitcher throw three strikes without taking a single cut at the ball. Three golden opportunities to at least advance a runner, get on base himself, or maybe even hit a home run, and he never moves the bat from his shoulder. The reason is simple. He saw himself striking out, being put out, or maybe hitting into a double play. He left his bat on his shoulder hoping for a walk, a free ride to first base.

It is even more disappointing to see a person in the ball game of life step up to the plate and never really take a cut at the ball. He is the biggest failure of all, according to Larry Kimsey, M.D., because he doesn't try. If you try and lose, you can learn from losing, which greatly reduces the loss. You learn nothing from expecting free "walks." These people serve as their own judge and jury and sentence themselves to a life in the prison of mediocrity. They never really get in the game of life and take an honest cut at the ball. Their self-image is that of failing or striking out. You cannot consistently perform in a manner that is inconsistent with the way you see yourself. It is a coach's job to show you that if you have anything less than a positive self-image, you are a "thief" and you are wrong in the way you feel about yourself.

To better understand this point, consider the stories of three thieves. The scene is a small neighborhood grocery store and the year is 1887. A distinguished-looking gentleman in his late fifties or early sixties is buying some turnip greens. He hands the clerk a 20-dollar bill and waits for his change. The clerk accepts the money and starts to place it in the cash drawer as she makes change. However, she notices the ink is coming off on her fingers, which are still wet from handling the turnip greens. She is shocked and pauses to consider what to do. After an instant of wrestling with the problem, she makes a decision. The customer is Emmanuel Ninger, a long-time friend, neighbor, and customer. Surely, he would not give her a bill that was anything less than genuine, so she gives him the change and he leaves.

Later, she has second thoughts, because 20 dollars was a lot of money in 1887. She sends for the police. One policeman is confident that the 20-dollar bill is the genuine article. The other is puzzled about the ink that rubbed off. Finally, curiosity combined with responsibility forces them to obtain a warrant to search Mr. Ninger's home. In the attic, they find the facilities for reproducing 20-dollar bills. As a matter of fact, they find a 20-dollar bill in the process of being made. They also find three portraits that Emmanuel Ninger painted. Ninger is an artist, and a good one. He is so good, he is hand-painting those 20-dollar bills. Meticulously, stroke by stroke, he applies the master's touch so skillfully that he is able to fool everyone until a quirk of fate in the form of the wet hands of a grocery store clerk exposes him. After his arrest, his portraits were sold at public auction for $16,000—more than $5,000 each. The irony of the story is, it took Emmanuel Ninger almost exactly the same length of time to paint a 20-dollar bill as it took him to paint a $5,000 portrait.

Yes, this brilliant and talented man was a thief in every sense of the word. Tragically, the person he stole the most from was Emmanuel Ninger. Not only could he have been a wealthy man if he had legitimately marketed his ability, but he could have brought so much joy and so many benefits to his fellow man in the process. He is on an endless list of those who steal from themselves when they steal from others.

A second thief is a man named Arthur Barry. He too was an unusual thief. He was a jewel thief who operated during the "roaring '20s." Barry gained an international reputation as possibly the most outstanding jewel thief of all time. He was not only a successful jewel thief, but also a connoisseur of the arts. As a matter of fact, he had become a snob and would not steal from "just anyone." Not only must his "prospects" have money and jewels for him to come calling, but their name must be listed among the top echelons of society. It became somewhat of a status symbol to have been called on and robbed by this "gentleman thief."

One night Barry was caught during a robbery and shot three times. With bullets in his body, splinters of glass in his eyes, and suffering excruciating pain, he made a not-too-unexpected statement, "I'm never going to do this again." Miraculously, he escaped and for the next three years remained free. Then, a jealous woman turned him in and Barry served an 18-year sentence. When he was released, he kept his word. He didn't go back to the life of a jewel thief. As a matter of fact, he settled in a small New England town and lived a model life. Local citizens honored him by making him the commander of a local veteran's organization.

Eventually, however, word leaked out that Arthur Barry, the famous jewel thief, was in their midst. Reporters from all over came to interview him. One young reporter got to the crux of the matter when he asked the most penetrating question of all. "Mr. Barry," he asked, "you stole from a lot of wealthy people during your years as a thief, but I'm curious to know if you remember the one man from whom you stole the most?" Barry, without a moment's hesitation, said, "That's easy. The man from whom I stole the most was Arthur Barry. I could have been a successful businessman, a baron on Wall Street, and a contributing member to society, but instead I chose the life of a thief and spent two-thirds of my adult life behind prison bars."

The third thief is you. You are a thief because any person who does not believe in himself and fully utilize his ability is literally stealing from himself, from his loved ones, and, in the process, because of reduced productivity, he also steals from society. Since no one would knowingly steal from himself, it's obvious that those who steal from themselves do it unwittingly. Nevertheless, the crime is serious because the loss is just as great as if it were deliberately done. The key point is that it is time for you to quit stealing from yourself.

DO: (15 MINUTES)

- Lead the group through the discussion questions found on the student worksheet.
- Review the word of the day. Ask a student to use it correctly in a sentence.

YOU ARE A THIEF—WORKSHEET

"There is no man living who isn't capable of doing more than he thinks he can do."
—Henry Ford

For discussion:

1. How can it be that when you steal from others, you are really stealing from yourself?

_____

_____

_____

_____

_____

2. How do you steal from yourself by not using your talents properly?

_____

_____

_____

_____

_____

3. What are some specific examples of how the time you waste represents theft in the following areas?

   • School_____

   • Athletics_____

Word of the Day: Potential—capacity for realization and development

THE SUCCESS INSTINCT—COACH'S NOTES

SAY: (5 MINUTES)

A squirrel born in the spring gathers nuts for a winter it has never before experienced. Why? The squirrel has within it a "success instinct." This instinct to live is built-in. Animals have only the most basic instincts of survival and reproduction.

If every living creature has this success instinct, certainly humans have it also. Humans have emotional and spiritual needs, as well as physical needs. Humans have a creative imagination. Humans are more than creatures; they are also creators. With your imagination, you can formulate a variety of goals. Humans alone can direct their success instinct through imagination.

You are not a machine, but within you the success instinct works just like a machine would. It is totally impersonal, meaning that it will work as a success instinct or a failure instinct to get you to the top or the bottom. It is totally and completely up to you. If you think of the human brain and nervous system as a machine, you will gain new insight into the whys and wherefores of human behavior.

This machine—your brain—is used for two areas of problem-solving:

- When the target, goal, or answer is known and the objective is to reach it or accomplish it
- When the target or answer is not known and the objective is to discover and locate it

A good metaphor for the first area is a self-guided torpedo. The target is known to be an enemy ship. The objective is to reach it. The torpedo must have a propulsion system to propel it forward in the direction of the target. The torpedo must be equipped with "sense organs" to stay on target. When it commits an error, it must correct itself and get back on course. The torpedo accomplishes its goal by going forward, making errors, and continually correcting them. It remembers its successes, forgets it failures, and repeats the successful actions. These actions become habits.

An example of the second area is recalling a name that has been temporarily forgotten. A scanner in your brain scans back through your stored memories until the correct name is recognized. It may be hours later, but the success instinct in you kept working to solve the problem.

You may marvel at the torpedo, but a greater marvel is the baseball player catching a fly ball. He follows the same procedures as the torpedo. To compute where the ball will fall, he takes into account the speed of the ball, wind, initial velocity, and rate of progressive decrease in velocity. Next, he must calculate how fast to run to arrive at just the right time. His success instinct does all this through the data fed into his computer through his sense organs—his eyes and ears. All computations are worked in a flash; the orders go to his leg muscles and he just runs.

The brain and nervous system form a machine *within* you to be used *by* you. The machine will run on the success instinct if you adhere to the following five principles:

- Have a target or goal. This goal must be thought of as already in existence, either in actual or potential form.
- Think in terms of end results. The machine will supply the means to reach the goal. Do not be discouraged if the means are not apparent.
- Do not be afraid of making mistakes or of temporary failure. The machine works by going forward, making mistakes, correcting errors, and continuing to move forward.
- Mentally correct yourself after each error. Skill-learning of any kind is accomplished by trial and error. After corrections are made, further learning and continual success are accomplished by forgetting the past errors and remembering the successes so that they can be repeated.
- Trust the machine to do its work and do not jam it up by becoming too concerned or too anxious about whether it will work or by attempting to force the machine's system through too much conscious effort. You must let it work rather than make it work. This trust is necessary because your success instinct operates below the level of consciousness and you are not always aware of what is going on beneath the surface.

Apply what you are learning and remember this quote from Ralph Waldo Emerson: "Do the thing, and you will have the power."

DO: (15 MINUTES)

- Lead the team in a discussion covering the questions found on the student worksheet.
- Review the word of the day. Ask a student to use it correctly in a sentence.

THE SUCCESS INSTINCT—WORKSHEET

"Who escapes duty, avoids a gain."

—Theodore Parker

For discussion:

1. What is the difference between the success instinct in animals and in humans?

   _____

   _____

   _____

2. How is the brain/nervous system similar to a machine?

   _____

   _____

   _____

3. Compare the outcome of a game to the torpedo example.

   _____

   _____

   _____

4. Develop in your own words a principle upon which the success instinct works.

   _____

   _____

   _____

Word of the Day: Instinct—a natural or inherent aptitude, impulse, or capacity

IMAGINATION IS YOUR KEY TO SUCCESS— COACH'S NOTES

SAY: (5 MINUTES)

People act or fail to act not because of will, but because of imagination.

Creative imagination is not something reserved for poets, philosophers, or inventors. Imagination can be seen in your every action. Imagination creates the picture on which your success instinct works. A human being always acts, feels, and performs in accordance with what he imagines to be true about himself and his environment. This statement is the basic and fundamental law of the mind.

Persuasive speakers, teachers, and coaches can convince their students and teams that they could do incredible things—and then watch them do it. Prophets of doom can convince their children, students, and players that no "good losers" exist—and then watch them lose. Plant a positive, winning picture in the mind and the mind goes to work to help the body complete the picture. But, plant a negative, losing picture in the mind and the mind goes to work to help the body complete the picture. That process is the normal operating procedure of the human brain and nervous system.

You act and feel, not according to what things are like, but according to the image your mind holds of what they are like. You have certain mental images of yourself, your world, and the people around you, and you behave as though these images are reality, rather than the things they represent. Realizing that your actions, feelings, and behavior are the result of your own image and beliefs gives you the power to change your self-image.

Mental pictures offer an opportunity to practice new traits, new skills, and new attitudes. This process is possible because the nervous system cannot tell the difference between an actual experience and one that is vividly imagined. If you picture yourself performing in a certain manner, it is nearly the same as the actual performance. Mental practice helps to make perfect.

Research Quarterly reports an experiment on the effects of mental practice on improving skill in sinking basketball free throws. The athletes in the experiment were divided into three groups, each of which was tested on the first and last day. One group actually practiced shooting free throws every day for 20 days. A second group engaged in no practice in between tests. The third group spent 20 minutes a day imagining that they were shooting at the basket. When they missed, they would imagine that they corrected their aim accordingly. The results were quite interesting. The first group improved 25 percent. The second group showed no improvement. The third group improved 23 percent.

Johnny Bulla, the professional golfer, once wrote that having a clear mental image of just where you wanted the ball to go and what you wanted it to do was more important than form in golf. Most of the pros, said Bulla, have one or more serious flaws in their form, yet they manage to shoot well. If you picture the end result, you see the ball going where you want it to go, you have the confidence to know that it is going to do what you want, and your subconscious takes over and directs your muscles correctly.

Successful men and women have long used mental pictures and rehearsal practice to achieve success. Napoleon, for example, practiced soldiering in his imagination for many years before he ever went on an actual battlefield.

Walter Payton once remarked that the key to success for him was being raised without TV. It forced him to develop an imagination. As a cowboy, he had to imagine the Indian that attacked. By using and developing his imagination, he imagined himself as a great NFL running back.

Instead of trying by conscious effort to do something by exerting sheer willpower—while always worrying and picturing all the things that are likely to go wrong—try simply relaxing as you picture the target that you really want to hit. Let your success instinct take over. Mentally picturing the desired end result literally forces you to use positive thinking. You are not relieved from effort and work, but your efforts are used to carry you forward toward your goal, rather than in the futile mental conflict that results when you want and try to do one thing, but picture yourself doing another.

DO: (15 MINUTES)

- Allow the students time to write out their individual answers to the questions on the student worksheet, and then have them share with the entire group or divide into smaller groups and discuss.
- Review the word of the day. Ask a student to use it correctly in a sentence.

Photo Credit: Lawrence Bestmann

LESSON #9

IMAGINATION IS YOUR KEY TO SUCCESS—
WORKSHEET

"Imagination rules the world."

—Napoleon Bonaparte

"Imagination, of all man's faculties, is the most God-like."

—Glen Clark

"The faculty for imagination is the great spring of human activity and the principal source of human improvement."

—Dugald Stewart

"You can imagine your future."

—Henry Kaiser

For discussion:

1. Choose one of the above quotes and write what it means to you.

   _____

   _____

   _____

   _____

2. Why is the fact that the nervous system cannot tell the difference between a real experience and a vividly imagined experience so vitally important?

   _____

   _____

   _____

3. How can you use this fact in practice?

   _____

   _____

   _____

Word of the Day: Envisage—to have or form the mental image of

REPAINTING THE PICTURE—COACH'S NOTES

SAY: (5 MINUTES)

Your actions are based on the fact that you believe what a person you trust says is true. From these truths and beliefs, you decide what it is that can and cannot be done. Most often, people do not doubt truths that have been with them since childhood—they simply act on them because they have decided that they are true. It is through conscious thinking and rational logic that you are able to use your success instinct.

The present and future depend on learning new habits and new ways of looking at old problems. The fact that past failures occurred does not mean that they must be re-examined to cause a personality change. All skill learning is by trial and error—making a trial, missing the mark, remembering the degree of error, and making corrections on the next trial—until a successful attempt is accomplished. The successful pattern is remembered for future trials. This statement is true of horseshoes, driving a car, playing golf, getting along sociably with other humans, or any other skill.

The failures, the negative experiences, do not inhibit, but rather contribute to, the learning process, as long as they are used properly. The negative experience has to be seen as a deviation from the goal.

Remember, your success instinct is totally impersonal. In other words, it will strive to reach whatever goal or end result you give it. If you dwell on the negative and constantly focus on failure, it changes from a success instinct to a failure instinct. It will work to accomplish whatever picture you paint for it.

Keep in mind that failure and negative experiences are simply steps to the positive attainment of goals. Failure is temporary. Failure is a verb denoting an action; it is never a noun. Things that have happened in the past have no power over the future. It is foolish to say, "Because I failed yesterday, I will fail tomorrow." The minute you stop giving power to the past, the past loses its power over you. Ignore past failures and "act as if it were impossible to fail." Determine to try to act as if the power and abilities are yours.

Ideas are not changed by willpower; they are changed by other ideas. Your beliefs exist because of some reason. Remember, both behavior and feelings spring from what you believe to be true, not from truth itself.

When faced with a belief that is holding you back, ask yourself these questions:
- Why do I believe that I can't?
- Is there a rational reason for such a belief?
- Could it be that I am mistaken in this belief?
- Would I come to the same conclusion about some other person in a similar situation?

Rational thinking takes the negative concept of worry and turns it into a positive one. When the golfer gets to the water hazard, he worries about the ball going in the water. He is painting a picture—an end result of what he expects the ball to do. When you worry, you are putting the negative end result into your computer and your success instinct will work until it realizes that end result. If that end result is the ball in the water, that is what your success instinct works to make happen.

Thomas Edison failed more than 10,000 times before he found the right filament to allow a light bulb to burn. But he never believed it was not there. He always had an end result in his mind, and therefore the success instinct kept him working 24 hours a day to accomplish the end result. He did not constantly paint the negative. Failure was temporary and brought him one step closer to success. In fact, he said, "Our greatest weakness lies in giving up. The most certain way to succeed is to always try just one more time."

DO: (15 MINUTES)

- Allow the students 10 minutes to work on the student worksheet individually. Then ask for volunteers to share what they learned in this session.
- Review the word of the day. Ask a student to use it correctly in a sentence.

REPAINTING THE PICTURE—WORKSHEET

"Doubt whom you will, but never yourself."

—Christian Bovee

For discussion:

1. Write down three beliefs that you have about yourself.

    _____

    _____

    _____

2. For each belief, ask yourself these questions:

    •   Why do I believe this?

    •   Is there a rational reason for this belief?

    •   Could I be mistaken in this belief?

    •   Would I come to the same conclusion about another person in a similar situation?

Word of the Day: Assertive—disposed to or characterized by boldness or confidence

RELAX AND LET THE SUCCESS INSTINCT WORK FOR YOU—COACH'S NOTES

SAY: (10 MINUTES)

Now that you have learned to focus on the end result you desire, relax and let your success instinct work for you. Remember, it is imperative that you give the success instinct a positive end result and, just as importantly, a passionate desire to reach that end result.

The conscious brain gives the success instinct within you a goal or a problem that must be solved. The success instinct then begins to work on that picture. As long as you keep the picture of the desired end result in mind, the success instinct will find a way to reach the goal or solve the problem.

William James said that modern man was too tense, too concerned for results, and too anxious, and he felt there was a better way. People need to free their minds from inhibitive influences. He said, "When once a decision is reached and execution is the order of the day, dismiss absolutely all responsibility and care about the outcome. Unclasp your intellectual and practical machinery and let it run for you." He wrote this back in 1899!

The secret of creative thinking and creative doing is our allowing your success instinct to work. Do not hinder it by trying too hard. It is well-known that when Thomas Edison was stymied by a problem, he would lie down and take a nap.

How many times have you tried to think of an answer, only to finally give up and then later, when you are not even thinking about the question, the answer came to you? Though you tried as hard as you could to solve the problem with conscious thought, it was not until you relaxed that the answer came. Even though you consciously gave up on finding the answer, your success mechanism continued to work "underground" until it found the answer.

This instinct works in the same way with skill learning. Skill in any performance, whether it be sports, playing a piano, or conversation, consists not of painfully and consciously thinking out each action, but of relaxing and letting the job do itself through you. Michael Jordan "flowed" with the game. Barry Sanders did not think about each move. They allowed the instincts within them to operate at top efficiency. They had the picture of what they wanted and they allowed their creative energy to get them the results. They were able to be so skilled only when they reached the point where they lost the conscious effort and turned the matter over to the success instinct.

Conscious effort "jams" the mechanism. The reason some football players are so awkward running ropes is that they are too concerned—too anxious—to do each drill by conscious effort. It is the same in a social setting. Some people are awkward because they are trying too hard. Every action or word is thought out. Everything is calculated.

Consequently, they seem stiff and awkward. If these people would let go and stop trying so hard they would act creatively and be themselves.

Consider the following four rules for freeing your success instinct:

❑ *Rule #1: Do your worrying before you develop your plan of action.*

Remember the advice of William James: "When once a decision is reached and execution is the order of the day, dismiss absolutely all responsibility and care about the outcome. Unclasp your intellectual and practical machinery and let it run for you." This process enables you to free your mind and perform better in all areas of life, including sports.

Many young people sign up for something and then start worrying about what is going to happen. You need to spend your time before you sign up making sure it is what you want, and then put your effort into enjoying the sport. Treat this decision just like an athletic contest. Do all your worrying and planning during the practices. Relax and allow your success instinct to work at game time. This process is also a great help in taking tests. Study hard, prepare hard, and then when you go in to take the test, relax and allow your success instinct to work.

❑ *Rule #2: Form the habit of consciously responding to the present moment.*

Play this play. Do not concern yourself with what will happen in the fourth quarter. Take care of right now. Play one play at a time. Many players have difficulty practicing because they are pacing themselves to do the entire practice. They concern themselves with what will be happening one hour from now. Take care of each drill, respond to the present. Don't try to predict or do the future until you have done the present.

❑ *Rule #3: Do one thing at a time.*

Many students try to watch TV and study. Studies have proven that this method of study is not effective. Your success instinct can help you do any job, perform any task, solve any problem. Think of yourself as giving a problem to your success instinct as a scientist gives a problem to a computer. Just as a computer cannot give the right answer if three difficult problems are mixed up and fed at the same time, neither can your success instinct. Ease off on the pressure. Stop trying to cram more than one job at a time into the machinery.

❑ *Rule #4: Relax while you work.*

Consider this story about a player who hated to practice and was really a pain for his coach. He finally came in about one week before spring football and told the coach that he was quitting. The coach took him home, as was team policy, to let his parents know of his decision. His dad informed the coach and the boy in no uncertain terms that he was not going to quit, that he would play whether he liked it or not. Needless to say, the coach was not anxious to be coaching a player that was being forced to play. He had been unpleasant before, and the coach figured it would be worse, though he could not have been more wrong. The athlete had a great spring, made the starting lineup, and even became a leader by the end of spring. The coach asked him, "Why such a change?" He told the coach that he decided if he was going to have to play, he was going to relax and have a good time. He said that prior to his dad's ultimatum he had always spent most of the day dreading practice and having to come, and then trying to get practice over with by doing as little as possible.

Once his dad had eliminated his "out," the boy just decided he wasn't going to worry anymore. He was going to relax and have a good time and he didn't care if he started or even played. He discovered, quite to his surprise, that he really enjoyed playing. He ended up being an All-District player on a state championship team.

DO: (10 MINUTES)

- Quickly review each of the four rules.
- Lead a discussion on Question #1.
- Ask for volunteers to share their answers to Question #2.
- Review the word of the day. Ask a student to use it correctly in a sentence.

Photo Credit: Darren McNamara/Getty Images Sport

RELAX AND LET THE SUCCESS INSTINCT WORK FOR YOU—WORKSHEET

LESSON #11

"Inspirations never go in for long engagements; they demand immediate marriage to action."

—Brendan Francis

List the four rules for freeing your success instinct:

-

-

-

-

For discussion:

1. Discuss each rule and apply it to you and your team.

   _____

   _____

   _____

   _____

2. Write down one thing you will do differently today because of this lesson.

   _____

   _____

   _____

   _____

Word of the Day: Brainstorm—a sudden clever idea

BE YOURSELF—COACH'S NOTES

SAY: (5 MINUTES)

Why does everyone love a baby? Certainly, it is not for what it can do, or what it knows. Perhaps it is because a baby displays no phoniness or hypocrisy. A baby is completely honest, exemplifying the dictum, "Be yourself." A baby is not in the least bit inhibited.

Every human being has the mysterious something called "personality." When you say a person has a good personality, what you really mean is that he has freed and released the creative potential within and is able to express his real self. Poor personality and inhibited personality are the same thing. Such a person does not allow the creative self inside to be expressed. He has inhibited the inner self. The word "inhibit" literally means to stop, prevent, prohibit, or restrain. Numerous symptoms of inhibited personality exist—e.g., shyness, timidity, self-consciousness, hostility, nervousness, and inability to get along with others.

Have you ever tried to thread a needle? What you notice is that you can hold the thread as still as a rock until you get close to the eye of the needle, and then you begin shaking. This shaking is called a "purpose tremor." It occurs when people try too hard or they are too careful when trying to do something.

Henry Ward Beecher once said, "I don't like these cold, precise, perfect people who in order not to speak wrong, never speak at all and in order not to do wrong, never do anything." People sometimes confuse criticism or excitement as reasons to stop. Because you are off the mark does not mean you stop. You simply change your course and then continue. Will Rogers said, "You might be on the right track, but if you just sit there you will get run over."

Most inhibitions are created because people are overly concerned with what others think. When this happens, they become too careful. When they try to monitor every word or action, they inhibit themselves from being who they are. The way to make a good impression on other people is to never consciously try to make a good impression on them.

Consider the following feedback signals, which can tell you whether you are off-course because of too *little* inhibition. If you catch yourself exhibiting these signals, you need to think more about the consequences before acting:

- You continually get yourself into trouble because of overconfidence
- You habitually "rush in where angels fear to tread"
- You habitually find yourself in hot water because of impulsive actions
- Projects backfire because you "do now, ask questions later"
- You can never admit you are wrong
- You are a loud talker

On the other hand, if you are shy around strangers, if you dread new and strange situations, if you feel inadequate, worry a lot, or feel self-conscious—these symptoms show that you have too much inhibition and that you are too careful in everything you do.

Whether you are too inhibited or not inhibited enough, the cure to help you be yourself is as follows:

- Speak your mind. State your opinion with confidence and be willing to change your mind when presented with new information.
- Stop criticizing yourself. The inhibited person continually indulges in critical self-analysis. After each action, he says to himself, "I wonder if I should have done that." After he says something, he says to himself, "Maybe I shouldn't have said that." Stop beating yourself up. Watch for this habit and stop it.
- Speak a little louder. Experiments have shown that you can exert up to 15 percent more strength and lift more weight if you will shout, grunt, or groan loudly as you perform the lift. The explanation for this phenomenon is that loud shouting disinhibits and allows you to exert all of your strength, including that which has been blocked off and tied up by inhibitions.
- Learn to express positive emotions. The inhibited person is as afraid of expressing good feelings as bad ones. If he expresses love, he is afraid he will be seen as soft. If he expresses friendship, he is afraid it will be seen as "apple-polishing." If he compliments someone, he is afraid they will think that he is after something. Don't be afraid to let people know that you like them.

DO: (15 MINUTES)

- Lead a discussion of Questions #1 and #2.
- Allow the students individual time to complete Question #3. You may ask for volunteers to share their answers.
- Review the word of the day. Ask a student to use it correctly in a sentence.

LESSON #12

BE YOURSELF—WORKSHEET

"Pretension almost always overdoes the original, and hence exposes itself."

—Hosea Ballou

For discussion:

1. What does inhibit mean? How have you inhibited yourself in the past?

   _____

   _____

   _____

2. Do you see yourself as a person with too little or too much inhibition?

   _____

   _____

   _____

3. Four cures are listed below to help you be yourself. Beside each cure, write a specific situation in which you will implement that action step.

   1. Speak your mind _____

   _____

   2. Stop criticizing yourself _____

   _____

   3. Speak a little louder _____

   _____

   4. Express positive emotions _____

   _____

Word of the Day: Pretension—an extravagant show; lavish display

HEALING EMOTIONAL SCARS—COACH'S NOTES

LESSON #13

SAY: (5 MINUTES)

When you receive a physical injury, such as a cut, your body forms scar tissue that is both tougher and thicker than the original flesh. The purpose of the scar tissue is to form a protective cover or shell—nature's way of ensuring against another injury in the same place.

People are inclined to do very much the same thing whenever they receive an emotional injury, when someone hurts them. They form emotional or spiritual "scars" for self-protection. They are very apt to become hardened of heart, calloused toward the world, and to withdraw within a protective shell.

Many people have inner emotional scars. These people have been hurt or injured by someone in the past. To guard against future injury from that source, they form an emotional scar to protect their egos. The scar tissue, however, not only protects them from the individual who originally hurt them, it "protects" them against all other human beings.

A man who has been hurt by one woman takes a vow never to trust any woman again. A child who has had his self-image ruined by a cruel parent or teacher may take a vow to never trust any authority in the future. The scar tissue can be so thick that it removes them from any relationships. When people cannot effectively deal with others, they cannot deal with themselves.

Usually, underneath the hard shell of the person who is constantly bragging, seems to hate all authority, and protests too much, is a soft, vulnerable person who wants to interact with others. However, he cannot get close to anyone because he will not trust anyone. Sometime in the past, he was hurt by a person important to him, and he dares not leave himself open to be hurt again. He always has his defenses up. To prevent further rejection and pain, he attacks first. His method of communication is always a put-down. He risks nothing. He drives away the very people who would love him.

The emotional scars have given this person a picture of being unwanted, unliked, and incompetent. He views the world in which he lives as a hostile place. He views relationships as combative and competitive, rather than as giving and cooperative. He doesn't try to get along. Instead, he tries to always be one up. He has trouble being charitable to others or himself. This player feels the player–coach relationship is a competition. He does not trust the coach, so he makes his own decisions on the importance of the drills and methods the coaches have for improvement. To cooperate and follow would be to trust and, due to his past, this player has a difficult time trusting the coach to help him achieve his goals.

Not only do people incur emotional wounds from others, most inflict wounds upon themselves. They beat themselves up with self-condemnation, remorse, and guilt. Remorse and regret are attempts to emotionally hide in the past. Guilt is trying to make something from the past. Since people cannot live in the past, they obviously cannot emotionally react appropriately to the past. What is past is past. You need to forgive, forget, and move on. Holding a grudge or reliving the past is neither helpful nor healthy. The important things are your present direction and your present goal.

"It matters not where you have been. All that matters is where you are going." This saying, which was used at a Boys' Home for years, simply meant to move forward, forget the past, and get excited about the future. In this same regard, one of the biggest mistakes you can make is to confuse your behavior with yourself (i.e., to conclude that because you did certain acts, it makes you a certain type of person).

Dr. Wendell Johnson, a leading authority on stuttering, believes that this sort of thing is the cause of stuttering. When a child stutters and the parents say, "He stuttered," chances are reduced that he will become a stutterer compared to if the parents had said, "He is a stuttered." This second response is much more likely to result in the child becoming a stutterer. These parents are confusing an action with a person. You make mistakes; you are not a mistake.

In a 20-year study of habits, it was found that in habit making, or breaking, it is essential that the person learn to stop blaming or condemning himself. If he is to change bad habits, he must see them as separate from his self-image. So, remember, you make mistakes. Mistakes don't make you anything.

As the body needs an outer layer to protect the vital organs, the self-image needs a protective covering to keep it productive. If your outer skin is too thick, you have no sense of feeling. It is undoubtedly the same with the inner-self. With too thick a covering, you have no feeling for people. To be truly happy in life, you must learn how to enjoy other people and let them into your life.

DO: (10 MINUTES)

- Allow the team a few minutes to individually answer Question #1. Some painful situations may arise that you will want to handle outside of this class.
- Discuss either in small work groups or as a big group Questions #2 and #3.
- Review the word of the day. Ask a student to use it correctly in a sentence.

HEALING EMOTIONAL SCARS—WORKSHEET

"What a man thinks of himself, that is what determines, or rather indicates, his fate."
—Henry David Thoreau

For discussion:

1. Do you have any emotional scars you have not dealt with? If yes, what do you need to do to get past those scars?

_____

_____

_____

_____

_____

2. How can living in the past affect your parents?

_____

_____

_____

_____

_____

3. What does the Boy's Home motto mean to you?

_____

_____

_____

_____

_____

Word of the Day: Destiny—a predetermined or inevitable course of events

THE GOOD PICTURE—COACH'S NOTES

SAY: (5 MINUTES)

One of the most effective means of helping people achieve a successful personality is to give them a graphic picture of what a successful personality looks like. Remember, the success instinct is a goal-striving instinct, and the first requirement for using it is to have a clear-cut picture or end result to shoot for. Success is not what you have achieved compared to others. Success is how much you use of what you have been given. Success is dealing effectively and appropriately with the environment and reality, and gaining satisfaction from reaching goals that are important to you.

An easy-to-remember picture of the successful personality is contained in the letters of the word "success" itself:

Sense of direction
Understanding
Courage
Charity
Esteem
Self-confidence
Self-acceptance

Consider each of the aforementioned components separately:

❑ *Sense of Direction*

You are like a bicycle. A bicycle maintains its poise and equilibrium only as it is going forward. The same is true of you. If you try to stop and just maintain your current position, you are never going to be successful. You are engineered as a goal-seeking mechanism. When you have no personal goals you are apt to go around in circle, feel lost, and find life aimless and purposeless. This lack of direction is evident in many young people who have not found a purpose. You are built to conquer the environment, solve problems, and achieve goals. You will find no real satisfaction or happiness in life without obstacles to conquer and goals to achieve. Young people who say that life is not worthwhile are really saying that they themselves have no personal goals that are worthwhile. To be successful, you need to find something important to you—and then go for it.

❑ *Understanding*

Understanding is the ability to see things from both sides; the ability, in most cases, to separate fact from opinion.

Fact: Two friends are whispering when you walk up. They suddenly stop talking.
Opinion: They must be talking about you.

Fact: Coach does not speak when you see him.
Opinion: Coach is mad at you.

You can take your opinions of these two facts and, if you allow them to, they can drive you to all sorts of actions that end up causing you more and more trouble. To be successful, you have to separate what is fact and what is opinion. You have to be able to see both sides of arguments, and you must be able to face the truth. Look for and seek out truth in all situations. Remember, you progress by correcting errors, remembering successes, and moving forward.

❑ *Courage*

Elbert Hubbard once remarked, "The greatest mistake a man can make is to be afraid to make one." And Sir Winston Churchill, the Prime Minister of England, said, "Courage is the first of human qualities because it is the quality which guarantees all the others." Nothing in this world is ever absolutely certain or guaranteed. More often than not, the difference between success and failure is not ability, but the willingness of the successful person to act. Courage is not just being heroic in battle; it is taking risks and acting in everyday life. Picture the most promising course and take it. If you wait until you are absolutely certain before you act, you will never do anything. Any time you act you can be wrong. You must daily have the courage to risk making mistakes, risk failure, and risk being humiliated. Once you begin moving, you can correct your course as you go. The safest place for a ship is in the harbor. Chances are it will not sink, but it will rust out and become ineffective twice as fast sitting in the harbor than if it were moving in the open sea. Don't put your ship in harbor. Step forward and start sailing. Have the courage to risk failure.

❑ *Charity*

Zig Ziglar once said, "You can have everything in life you want if you will just help enough other people get what they want." What does that mean to you? Maybe you will set as your goal to make your coach the "Coach of the Year." If you accomplish that goal and give the coach what he wants, you will likely get what you want as well. If your coach is the "Coach of the Year," you will have played on a very successful team, if not a championship team. (*Note*: Use an example appropriate from your sport here.) If you are an offensive lineman and you really want to make All-District, set your goal to help your running back get 1,000 yards. If the running back gets 1,000 yards, you will very likely get all the honors you want. If you will help all your teammates get through practice in a positive way, you will get everything out of practice you want. If you carry your teammates to the top of the mountain, you are at the peak as well.

❑ *Esteem*

To paraphrase St. Augustine, man will marvel at the sun, the stars, the forests, and the rainbows, and will pass by the greatest miracle of all (man himself) without even a notice. The word "esteem" literally means to appreciate the worth of something. People who have lost their sight, hearing, or mobility because of negligence have sued and won millions of dollars. Would you trade your eyes for a million dollars? Would you trade your ability to move, no matter how slow or awkward you think you are, for a million dollars?

The appreciation of your own worth is not conceit, unless you assume you made yourself and should get all of the credit. By the way, did you know conceit is the only sickness that makes everyone sick except the one who has it? Do not downgrade the product because you haven't used it correctly. Don't be like the schoolboy who says, "This typewriter can't spell."

❑ *Self-Confidence*

Build upon successes. Start with little things. Remember your successes, not your failures. The human brain works best with this method. Practice improves skill and success in basketball, golf, or horseshoe pitching, not because repetition has any value in itself. Practice does not make perfect. Practice makes permanent. Remember your successes and forget your failures after you correct them and move on. Use errors and mistakes as a way to learn, and then dismiss them from your mind. Recall the feelings that success brings.

❑ *Self-Acceptance*

No success is possible until you accept yourself. The most miserable people are the ones who are always trying to be somebody they are not. You do not need to change. You simply need to reprogram yourself from false beliefs, relax, and be yourself. You are not your mistake. Accept the fact that you will make mistakes as you constantly move forward.

DO: (15 MINUTES)

- Allow the students five minutes to work individually and then ask them to share their answers in small groups or with the entire team.
- Review the word of the day. Ask a student to use it correctly in a sentence.

THE GOOD PICTURE—WORKSHEET

"Success is simple. Do what is right, the rightway, at the right time."
—Arnold Glasgon

For discussion:

In your own words, write a short definition of each of the components of success:

Sense of direction: _____

_____

Understanding: _____

_____

Courage: _____

_____

Charity: _____

_____

Esteem: _____

_____

Self-confidence: _____

_____

Self-acceptance: _____

_____

Word of the Day: Evaluation—a careful examination; appraisal

BECOMING THE WINNER—COACH'S NOTES

SAY: (5 MINUTES)

Harry S. Truman once remarked, "A winner is the one who makes opportunities of crises. A loser is the one who makes crises of his opportunities." It is not always the baseball player with the best batting average that is called upon to pinch hit in a tough spot. It is the one who is known to come through in the clutch. One salesperson may be unable to speak in the presence of an important client, while another salesperson may sell enthusiastically in the identical situation. Some students do well in day-to-day class work, but find their minds blank when taking an examination. Other students do average in class work, but excel on important examinations.

The difference between all of these people is not some inherent quality, but rather a matter of how they respond to crisis situations.

- For something to be a crisis, it must have three factors:
- It must be happening to you.
- It must be occurring right now.
- It must be, in your opinion, a make-or-break situation.

To perform well in a crisis, you need to first learn certain skills and practice them without pressure. Then, you need to respond to the crisis with an aggressive rather than defensive attitude, while keeping your positive goal in mind. Lastly, you need to learn to evaluate so-called crisis situations in their true perspective. You do this by not making mountains out of mole hills, or reacting as if every small challenge were a matter of life or death.

What does it mean to practice without pressure? Some kids are taught to swim by being thrown into a lake or river. They learned how to swim, but not correctly. The crude, inept stroke that they use to keep from drowning becomes fixed. If they were placed in a situation that required them to swim a long distance, the method of swimming they learned under real pressure would probably not be good enough to keep them from drowning.

Laboratory animals have been placed in a maze. When they were in a nonstressful environment they learned three times as quickly as animals who were in a life-threatening environment. The second set of animals found that it was three times as difficult to learn the maze.

(*Note*: Use an appropriate example from your sport.) A perfect example of this phenomenon is learning a two-point play in football. Every football team learns the play in practice during the week. The team practices it daily and weekly until they get into the game and must have two points to win. The team knows what it will do and has practiced for just that moment. They have practiced responding without pressure. They do not notice the pressure because their focus is on the execution of the play. If they had not practiced this play, the pressure of the situation would be the focus.

A crisis situation can bring you unknown power. Many people have made the mistake of misinterpreting the feeling of excitement as fear and anxiety. Any normal person becomes excited or nervous in a crisis situation. Until you direct this energy toward a goal, it is not fear, anxiety, courage, confidence, or anything more than a hyped-up supply of emotional steam in your boiler. It is *not* a sign of weakness. It is a sign of additional strength to be used in any way you choose. Jack Dempsey used to get so nervous before a fight that he couldn't shave. He did not interpret this nervousness as fear. He used the excitement to put extra power in his punches.

People are the ones who choose labels for their reactions. If you run away, it was fear; if you stay and fight, it was courage. It is up to you. It has been proven thousands of times that you have more power when you are excited. People have picked up automobiles to save loved ones. When the mind labels a situation as a crisis, the body reacts with extra power. Then, all you must do is use the power.

Ask yourself, what is the worst that can possibly happen? Football coach Bum Phillips once said, "The worst they can do is fire me. They can't shoot and eat me."

Sometimes, when you think of the worst thing that could happen, you will realize that a situation is not as critical as you thought. Many people spend their lives making mountains out of mole hills. A man who goes for a job interview thinking he doesn't have the job before he goes in, is no worse off after being turned down than he was before he went in for the interview. You need to remember that within each of you is a success instinct. Paint the picture, the desired end result, and your success instinct will work until it is reached. Use the crisis to make yourself perform as a winner.

DO: (15 MINUTES)

- Lead the team through a discussion of the questions on the student worksheet.
- Review the word of the day. Ask a student to use it correctly in a sentence.

BECOMING THE WINNER—WORKSHEET

"Zeal will do more than knowledge."

—William Hazlitt

For discussion:

1. What does the Harry Truman quote mean to you?

_____

_____

_____

_____

2. The three steps to responding well to crises are listed below. How can you use each of them in your life?

   • Practice without pressure: _____

   _____

   • Use the power of a positive attitude: _____

   _____

   • Evaluate the crisis. What is the worst that can possible happen? _____

   _____

3. List two opportunities that you will have in the near future. How will you respond to them in a positive manner?

   _____

   _____

   _____

Word of the Day: Zeal—enthusiastic and intensive interest, as in a cause or ideal; ardor

CHANGING THE SELF-IMAGE (PART 1)— COACH'S NOTES

Note: Be sure to read the student worksheet and the accompanying information before class.

SAY: (5 MINUTES)

Your self-image is a golden key to living a better life because of two important discoveries. The first discovery is that all of your actions, feelings, and behaviors are always consistent with your self-image. In short, you will act like the sort of person you perceive yourself to be. In addition, you literally cannot act otherwise, in spite of all of your conscious efforts or will power. The man who perceives himself to be a failure will find some way to fail, in spite of all his good intentions. The self-image is the foundation upon which your entire personality and your behavior are built. Your experiences, therefore, seem to verify and strengthen your self-image. A vicious or a beneficial cycle is then set up.

When people try to lose weight, they work to physically take off pounds. Many are successful for a short period, and then regain the lost weight. The problem is that they still have the picture of themselves as fat. When Zig Ziglar decided to lose weight, he cut out an advertisement for men's underwear. Obviously, the model for men's underwear was not overweight. Ziglar put the picture on his bathroom mirror. What he was doing was changing the picture in his mind to see himself as the slim Zig Ziglar. Ziglar lost the 37 pounds and has kept it off because he changed his mental picture from a fat person to a slim model.

One of the reasons it can seem so difficult to change the picture is that most efforts to change are aimed at the outer self, rather than the inner self. The problem is that most people use positive thinking to change some particular habit or character defect. "I will catch the ball." Positive thinking without changing the picture cannot work. The action has to be consistent with the picture.

The second important discovery about self-image is that it can be changed. You are *what* and *where* you are because of what has gone into your mind. You can change these things by changing what goes into your mind. If self-image is formed from past experiences and positive thinking doesn't work, how can you change your self-image? How can you visualize successful experiences without actually experiencing the success? A remarkable discovery allows you to do this. This point is the key to changing your self-image.

The body cannot tell the difference between a real experience and an experience that is *vividly* imagined.

A prisoner of war was in isolation for five and a half of the seven years he was confined. He saw no one, talked to no one, and was unable to perform a normal routine of physical activity. For the first few months, he did virtually nothing but hope and pray for his release. Then he realized he had to take some positive steps if he was going to retain his sanity and stay alive. He selected his favorite golf course and started playing golf in his cage. In his own mind, he played a full 18 holes every day. He played them to the last minute detail. He "saw" himself dressed in his golfing clothes as he stepped up to the first tee. He visualized every weather condition in which he played. He "saw" the exact size of the tee box, the grass, the trees, the birds, and all of the golf course. He "saw" in minute detail the exact way he held his left hand on the club and the way he put his right hand on the club. He carefully lectured himself on keeping his left arm straight. He cautioned himself about taking the backswing slowly and easily while remembering to keep his eye on the ball. He visualized the flight of the ball down the center of the fairway. He watched it fly through the air, hit the ground, and roll until it came to a stop at the exact spot he selected.

Seven days a week for the remaining years he played 18 holes of perfect golf. Not once did he ever miss a shot. Not once did the ball ever stray out of the cup. The experiences were imagined so vividly by the mind that the body did not know it was not real. When he actually did play golf after a seven-year absence, his image of himself as a golfer had been completely changed by the use of his imagination. Prior to his imprisonment, he was a weekend golfer who generally shot in the nineties. The first time back on the course, he shot a sparkling 74.

The second illustration is a little more serious than playing a great game of golf. Two psychologists with the Veterans Administration in Los Angeles reported that some mental patients can improve their lot and perhaps shorten their stay in hospitals just by imagining that they are normal. Dr. Harry M. Grayson and Dr. Leonard B. Olinger told the American Psychological Association that they tried the idea on 45 men hospitalized with psychiatric problems. They were asked to take a test and answer the questions as they would if they were typical, well-adjusted people on the outside. "Three-fourths of them turned in improved test performances, and some of the changes for the better were dramatic," the psychologists reported.

For these patients to answer the questions "as a typical, well-adjusted person" would answer, they had to imagine how a typical, well-adjusted person would act. They had to imagine themselves in the role of a well-adjusted person. Doing so was enough to cause them to begin "acting like" and "feeling like" well-adjusted people.

The late Dr. Albert Edward Wiggam called your mental picture of yourself "the strongest force within you." If you can imagine yourself sane, then you can provide yourself with successful experiences to change a self-image that is wrong.

DO: (15 MINUTES)

- Ask the group what they learned and how they think they can apply the information in their lives.
- Hand out the copy of the student worksheet and go over the idea of the 30-minute practice sessions.

- The next two lessons incorporate these practice sessions.
- Review the word of the day. Ask a student to use it correctly in a sentence.

INFORMATION JUST FOR COACHES

In 1977, the author (Dennis Parker) taught the following concept to a group of offensive linemen on his team at Southeast Missouri University. In his own words, the results were dramatic: "I did not notice any appreciable difference and was discouraged at the time because during the practice sessions I felt some linemen were using it as nap time. That next fall we began two-a-days and the first day we were in pads we had a one-on-one drill. We had an outstanding athlete playing on the defensive line named Alex Clinton, who had been All-Conference the year before and had thoroughly dominated all my linemen in the spring. He was, of course, first in line for the defense. Boyd Paulsmeyer jumped to be the first of our group. Boyd was probably going to be a starter, but he was at best a mediocre player. I was surprised that he jumped in to challenge Alex. I would also add that the head coach was the defensive line coach, so all odds were stacked in the defense's favor. The defensive line coach (head coach) gave the signal when to fire out (always on the first sound) and there was no ballcarrier to tackle. Obviously, I expected Boy to get beat, get over it, and move to the next player where we had a better chance.

The coach called the cadence. Boyd Paulsmeyer fired out as never before. He had his head up, back was flat; he exploded into Alex, rolled his hips, moved his feet, pushed Alex back, and pinned him on the ground. Everyone except Boyd Paulsmeyer was in total shock. Alex and his coach wanted a rematch. I wanted to quit while we were ahead. Boyd seemed anxious for the rematch. Same scenario—same result. I had believed Alex had slipped the first time. After the third match, all with the same results, I came to the only conclusion: I was a great coach!

Sitting in the locker room after practice, I asked Boyd how he did what he had done. What had he done to make himself such an improved player? His reply was a great lesson for me, "I did the lifting and running program you gave me," he said, "but every night when I got in bed I spent 30 minutes visualizing what I just did, down to the very last detail." Boyd Paulsmeyer blocked Alex Clinton every night that summer. What he did on the first day was something he had done every night that summer. Boyd Paulsmeyer became an All-Conference tackle for Southeast Missouri because of this concept. He had always been a hard worker, but he also learned to use his imagination to visualize and to see the end result. He had gone as far as the physical would take him. His mind and the use of this concept to change his "picture" would make him the best offensive tackle I had ever coached."

The key point to remember is that changing a person's self-image can produce exceptional results. Practice the experience. It may change one player from mediocrity to greatness.

LESSON #16

CHANGING THE SELF-IMAGE (PART 1)— WORKSHEET

Please read the following and commit to practicing for 30 minutes today.

"Hold a picture of yourself long and steadily enough in your mind's eye and you will be drawn toward it," said Dr. Henry Emerson Fosdick. "Picture yourself vividly as defeated and that alone will make victory impossible. Picture yourself vividly as winning and that alone will contribute immeasurably to success. Great living starts with a picture, held in your imagination, of what you would like to do or be."

Your present self-image is built upon the picture you have of yourself. This picture grew out of interpreting and evaluating your past experiences. You should now use the same method to build a healthy self-image. Set aside a period of 30 minutes each day when you can be alone and undisturbed. Close your eyes and exercise your imagination.

The important thing is to make your picture as vivid and detailed as possible. You want your mental picture to approximate actual experiences as much as possible. The way to do this is to pay attention to small details, sights, sounds, and objects in your imagined environment. Details of the imagined environment are all important. In this exercise, for all practical purposes, you are creating a practice experience. If your imagination is vivid and detailed enough, your imagined practice is equivalent to an actual experience, insofar as your nervous system is concerned.

The next important thing to remember is that during this 30-minute period you see yourself acting and reacting appropriately, successfully, and ideally. It doesn't matter how you acted yesterday. You do not need to try to have faith that you will act in the same way tomorrow. Your nervous system will take care of that in time, if you continue to practice. See yourself acting, feeling, and "being" as you want to be. Do not say to yourself, "I am going to act this way tomorrow." Just say to yourself, "I am going to imagine myself acting this way now—for 30 minutes—today."

Imagine how you would feel if you were already the sort of personality you want to be. If you have been shy and timid, see yourself moving among people with ease and poise and feeling good because of it. See yourself playing the game down to the smallest detail. See the crowd and the scoreboard. Play the game in its entirety. See yourself being the hero, making the plays.

This experience builds new "memories" or stored data into your midbrain and central nervous system. It builds a new image of self. After practicing it for a time, you will be surprised to find yourself acting differently, more or less automatically and spontaneously. You will then be feeding on positive experiences instead of negative experiences.

CHANGING THE SELF-IMAGE (PART 2)— COACH'S NOTES

Note: No stories or student worksheets are used in this lesson. It is intended to be a practice session.

DO:

*   Go over the practice exercise instructions again from the Lesson #16 worksheet.
*   Let the students get in a relaxed position.
*   Give them a chance to lie down, if possible.
*   Reinforce how important it is to visualize the positive end result.

Discipline is essential. Students cannot take a nap. Tell them to use this time for "practice experience." Teach them how to use the technique so that they will be able to do it at home. Once they learn how, the best time to do this is the 30 minutes at night when they first get into bed. No radio or TV—30 minutes "imagining" the desired end result.

The practice sessions, Lessons #17 and #18, are probably the two most important assignments in the entire mental-training program.

CHANGING THE SELF-IMAGE (PART 3)— COACH'S NOTES

Note: No stories or student worksheets are used in this lesson. It is intended to be a practice session.

DO:

*   Go over the practice exercise instructions again from the Lesson #16 worksheet.
*   Let the students get in a relaxed position.
*   Give them a chance to lie down, if possible.
*   Reinforce how important it is to visualize the positive end result.

Discipline is essential. Students cannot take a nap. Tell them to use this time for "practice experience." Teach them how to use the technique so that they will be able to do it at home. Once they learn how, the best time to do this is the 30 minutes at night when they first get into bed. No radio or TV—30 minutes "imagining" the desired end result.

TEN PRACTICAL STEPS FOR CHANGING THE SELF-IMAGE (PART 1)—COACH'S NOTES

SAY: (5 MINUTES)

Note: The next three lessons cover 10 steps anyone can take to improve their self-image.

❑ *Step #1: Take an inventory of what you have.*

A woman in Gary, Indiana, received one million dollars because a drug had caused her to lose her sight. In California, another woman was awarded one million dollars because of a back injury incurred in an airplane accident. Doctors say she will never walk again. How would you like to swap places with either of these ladies? The chances are good that if you can see and you can walk, you would not even consider doing so, which makes you worth at least two million dollars.

People very often marvel at the stars, the planets, the majestic beauty of the mountains, rivers, and plains, and then pass over the most marvelous creation of all—the human being. No one quite like you exists. Original paintings sell because they are unique—one of a kind. You are one of a kind—unique in many ways.

Consider the following: If you had the only car in town, you would have an extremely valuable possession, unless you parked it in the garage and never used it. You do have the only *you* in existence—now get out of the garage and use the talents you have been given. Look at yourself scientifically. You have the capacity between your ears to store more information than is in the Library of Congress. If you were to build a computer with your brain's capabilities, it would cost millions of dollars, be larger than the Empire State Building, and require more electricity than a city of thousands. The real kicker is that once they got this computer built, it still could not originate or imagine one single thought or concept. You might say, "If I am so smart, why is it that I am not doing so well?" See if story fits you:

A number of years ago, oil was discovered on property that belonged to an elderly man. All of his life, he had lived in poverty, but the discovery of oil allowed him to live as a wealthy man. One of the first things he did was buy himself a huge new automobile. He bought an Abraham Lincoln stovepipe hat, a tuxedo with a bow tie, and completed his outfit with a big black cigar. Every day, he would drive into the hot, dusty little town that was nearby. He wanted to see everyone and be seen by everyone. He was a friendly old soul, so when riding through town he would turn all the way around and speak to folks. Interestingly enough, he never ran into anybody or over anybody. The reason was simple. Directly in front of that big, beautiful automobile, two horses were pulling it. Local mechanics said that nothing was wrong with the car's ignition. Inside the car were "hundreds of horses"—ready, willing, and raring to go, but the old man was using the two on the outside.

Many people make the mistake of looking outside to find two horsepower when they should look inside, where they have hundreds. Psychologists say that this ratio is about equal to the ability you have to the ability you use. In other words, you use only 2 to 5 percent of your ability.

Someone once stated to have you must do, and to do you must be. To extend that concept to schoolwork, to have you must do *work* (homework, study, classroom assignments) and to *work* you must be *interested*. It is not a lack of intelligence or brain power that causes you to fail. It is a lack of interest. Some players can learn an intricate offense and adjust during a heated game, and then when they make less than satisfactory grades tell the coach that they are not smart. It is the old excuse—"This typewriter cannot spell." They were using the horses on the outside and not using the power they had on the inside. All they needed to do was get interested and they would not have had problems with their schoolwork.

DO: (15 MINUTES)

* Lead the team through a discussion of Questions #1 and #2, leaving five minutes at the end of class for students to individually answer Question #3.
* Review the word of the day. Ask a student to use it correctly in a sentence.

Photo Credit: Elsa/Getty Images Sport

TEN PRACTICAL STEPS FOR CHANGING THE SELF-IMAGE (PART 1)—WORKSHEET

"It is more than probable that the average man could, with no injury to his health, increase his efficiency fifty percent."

—Walter Dill Scott

For discussion:

1. What percentage of your potential are you using? How can you improve this percentage?

_____

_____

2. To have you must do work, and to do work you must be interested. How can you make yourself more interested in the things you must do?

_____

_____

3. Step #1 is to take an inventory of yourself. Complete these lists to begin taking action on this step.

PHYSICAL		MENTAL		SPIRITUAL	
Strengths	Weaknesses	Strengths	Weaknesses	Strengths	Weaknesses

Word of the Day: Efficiency—acting effectively with a minimum of waste or effort

TEN PRACTICAL STEPS FOR CHANGING THE SELF-IMAGE (PART 2)—COACH'S NOTES

LESSON #20

SAY: (5 MINUTES)

In the last lesson, you looked at the first step a person could take to improve his self-image. What was it? (*Note*: Take an inventory of yourself.) This lesson looks at five additional steps in that regard.

❏ *Step #2: Make up—dress up—go up.*

The way you look on the outside has a definite bearing on how you feel and see yourself on the inside. Fewer discipline problems occur on school picture day when the students dress up than on any other day of the year. Maxwell Maltz, the famous plastic surgeon, once said that when you change the outside picture, you most frequently change the inside picture. Be your own plastic surgeon. Make up and dress up on the outside so you can go up on the inside.

❏ *Step #3: Regularly read stories of people who overcame great odds to succeed.*

Read the biographies and autobiographies of men and women who got a great deal out of life by making contributions to life. It would be difficult, if not impossible, to read the life stories of Henry Ford, Abraham Lincoln, Thomas Edison, Andrew Carnegie, Booker T. Washington, and others, and not be inspired. Anybody who reads the story of Eartha White, daughter of an ex-slave, will be inspired to do more with his life. When you relate to these stories and see others succeeding, you visualize yourself doing the same thing. Remember, you are *what* you are and *where* you are because of what has gone into your mind. You can change these things by changing what goes into your mind.

❏ *Step #4: Listen to speakers, teachers, and ministers who build mankind.*

When you hear great speakers, such as Paul Harvey, Robert Schuller, or Billy Graham, you will get a lift in many ways. As a rule of thumb, you are safe to assume that any book, speaker, movie, TV program, or recording that builds mankind will build you and your self-image.

❏ *Step #5: Begin with a series of short steps.*

One reason many people never attempt new things is fear of failure. If possible, start any new venture with a phase or portion you are confident you can handle, and then transfer the initial accomplishment from one area of success to another. Don't be disappointed if you do not gain self-confidence overnight. Remember, you have probably been making an overdraft on the bank of confidence all of your life. Realistically, you cannot expect to bring your account up-to-date in one day. The longer and more regularly you take the necessary steps and follow the recommended procedures, the bigger your account in the confidence bank of healthy self-image will be—and the bigger the confidence account, the greater the accomplishment.

❑ *Step #6: Join the smile, handshake, and compliment club.*

When you smile at someone and they smile back, you automatically feel better. Even if they don't smile back, you will feel better because you know the most destitute person in the world is the one without a smile. You immediately become richer by giving that person your smile. The same thing goes for a compliment. When you sincerely compliment a person or extend him a courtesy, he is going to receive a direct benefit and like himself better. It is impossible for you to make someone feel better and not feel better yourself.

One of the best ways to make anyone else feel better is to spread optimism and good cheer. You can do this almost instantly in your daily exchanges with associates and family. When someone says, "Hi, how are you doing?" give them a big, cheerful, "Super good, but I'll get better!" If you don't feel that good, it's safe to say you want to feel that way, and even safer to say that if you claim the feeling, you will soon have the feeling.

DO: (15 MINUTES)

- Ask for volunteers to share their answers to Question #1.
- Give each person a chance to think of one positive thing about the person on his right. (The goal is for everyone in the room to leave with positive feedback, so make sure that each person is "assigned" someone.)
- Ask the students to write the positive thing on a piece of paper, sign it, and give it to the person.
- After each person has had a chance to read their positive note, discuss Question #4.
- Review the word of the day. Ask a student to use it correctly in a sentence.

TEN PRACTICAL STEPS FOR CHANGING THE SELF-IMAGE (PART 2)—WORKSHEET

"Happiness is someone to love, something to do, and something to hope for."
—Chinese Proverb

For discussion:

1. Briefly give a report on someone you have read about who has overcome great odds to become successful.

_____

_____

_____

_____

2. On a separate sheet of paper, write at least one positive thing about the person on your right. Remember to be sincere. Write "I like (fill in the person's name), because (write the positive thing you like in this person)."

_____

_____

_____

_____

3. How did it feel to give the "I like" piece of paper? To get one?

_____

_____

_____

_____

Word of the Day: Victory—success in a struggle against an obstacle or opponent

TEN PRACTICAL STEPS FOR CHANGING THE SELF-IMAGE (PART 3)—COACH'S NOTES

SAY: (5 MINUTES)

This lesson features the final four of the 10 steps for improving your self-image.

❏ *Step #7: Do something for someone else.*

For this step to be effective, you must accept no compensation and the person you assist should not be in a position to do anything for you in return. If you will do something for someone who is unable to return the favor, you will get a lot more than you can possibly give. In many cases, what you give will mean much to the recipient, but the feeling you get when you do something for someone who cannot do for themselves is indescribable. You will realize that you are truly fortunate, that you do have a lot to be thankful for, that you can make a contribution, and that you are, in fact, somebody. In short, you will stand tall in your own eyes. Charles Dickens said it best: "No one is useless in this world who lightens the burden of it to anyone else."

❏ *Step #8: Carefully choose the people you run around with.*

Deliberately associate with people of a high moral character who look on the bright side of life, and the benefits will be enormous. Pick out those people who are enthusiastic about life and some of the enthusiasm will rub off on you. Remember, you acquire much of the thinking, mannerisms, and characteristics of the people you are around. This fact is true whether the people around you are good or bad. Even your IQ is affected by the people with whom you associate. In the July, 1976, issue of *Success Unlimited*, this story was told:

"In the Kibbutz in Israel, evaluations revealed that the average IQ of the Oriental Jewish children was 85, while it was 105 for the European Jewish children. This 'proves' that the European Jewish children were 'smarter' than the Oriental Jewish children—or does it? After four years in the Kibbutz, where the environment was positive, the motivation was excellent, and the dedication to learning and growth was substantial, the average IQ leveled off to the same number—115. That's exciting. When you associate with the right people with a positive, moral outlook on life, you greatly enhance your chance of being successful. Surround yourself with winners and you won't have a choice but to be a winner yourself."

❏ *Step #9: To build a healthy self-image, you must avoid certain things.*

Literally everything that goes into your mind has an effect and is permanently recorded. It either builds and prepares you for the future or it tears down and reduces your possibilities for accomplishment in the future. Pornography is an excellent example of something that diminishes you as a human being. Psychologists say that three viewings of an X-rated film or television program have the same psychological, emotional, and destructive impact in your mind as one physical experience. The people who see these shows are in agreement. They are sexually stimulated and view themselves with less respect. The reason is simple: These films or programs present mankind at its worst and when you see your fellow man degraded, you, in effect, see yourself degraded. It is impossible to view mankind at its worst and not feel that your own value has diminished, and you can neither be nor do any better than you think you are. Ironically, most X-rated films are advertised as "adult" entertainment for "mature" audiences. On the other hand, most psychologists agree that they are juvenile entertainment for immature and insecure audiences.

This powerful imagination of yours, when applied to the nightly TV programming, is devastating. Nighttime programming fare features everything from incest and adultery to trial marriage and wife-swapping. When you allow this garbage to enter your mind, it affects your reasoning and decision-making. The choices that you make will determine if you are a success or a failure.

❑ *Step #10: Learn from successful failures.*

The list of successful failures is extensive, for example Ty Cobb and Babe Ruth. Ty Cobb was thrown out more times trying to steal a base than any man in baseball history. Babe Ruth is among the all-time leaders in strikeouts. Yet nobody considers either of these two men failures. Everyone remembers their successes.

Other notable examples in this regard also exist. Thomas Edison's teacher called him a dunce, and he later failed more than 10,000 times in his effort to perfect the incandescent light. Albert Einstein failed a course in math. Henry Ford was broke at age 40. Walt Disney went broke seven times and had a nervous breakdown before he became successful. In reality, these people (and many other individuals like them) succeeded simply because they kept at it.

Former President Calvin Coolidge once said, "Nothing in the world can take the place of persistence. Talent will not. Nothing is more common than unsuccessful men with talent. Genius will not. Unrewarded genius is almost a proverb. Education alone will not. The world is full of educated derelicts. Persistence and determination alone are omnipotent."

DO: (15 MINUTES)

- Lead a discussion covering the questions found on the student worksheet.
- Review the word of the day. Ask a student to use it correctly in a sentence.

TEN PRACTICAL STEPS FOR CHANGING THE SELF-IMAGE (PART 3)—WORKSHEET

"Have patience with all things, but chiefly have patience with yourself. Do not lose courage in considering your own imperfections, but instantly set about remedying them—every day begin the task anew."

—St. Francis de Sales

For discussion:

1. What can you do this week for someone else where you do not expect anything in return? When will you do it?

_____

_____

_____

2. List your favorite TV shows and complete the chart.

TV Show	Positive, beneficial aspects of the showshow	Negative, harmful aspects of the show
_____	_____	_____
_____	_____	_____
_____	_____	_____
_____	_____	_____
_____	_____	_____
_____	_____	_____

3. Name a "successful failure" that you know. What can you learn from him or her?

_____

_____

_____

Word of the Day: Purity—free from contaminants or faults; clean

CHARACTER

Photo Credit: Harry How/Getty Images Sport

"A man's character is his fate."

—Heraclitus

Chapter 5

DO YOU HAVE THE CHARACTER TO HANDLE ADVERSITY?—COACH'S NOTES

SAY: (5 MINUTES)

Adversity is a reality of life. You are never really sure when adversity will come or how long it will stay, but the way each human being handles the difficult situations in his life is a direct reflection of the character he possesses. The real test of a person does not come when everything is going well. The real test of a person comes after adversity has struck and he overcomes and conquers it.

Adversity builds character. It forces you to analyze yourself to see what went wrong and to correct your mistakes so you can improve. When you lose or are faced with a problem, you have two options: You can quit and walk away or you can stay and meet the challenge head-on. When you face adversity, it is important that you face the situation immediately. Do not put it off, hoping the problem will go away. Great athletes have the ability and courage to look adversity in the eye and turn it into success.

Champions do this all the time. Timing is the important thing when facing adversity. By analyzing yourself immediately, you will discover your weaknesses and work to improve them. How you handle your losses determines whether you are a winner or a loser. Losers won't admit their mistakes. Their solution is to feel sorry for themselves.

Winners are seldom discouraged. They have weak moments, as we all do, but they come fighting back. Winners treat adversity as a challenge or a test, not as a threat. Competition is a learning opportunity, regardless of outcome. Adversity makes winners work harder and accomplish even more.

Successful people are not afraid to fail. They accept their failures and continue on, knowing that failure is a natural consequence of trying. They go from failure to failure, until, at last, success is theirs. The law of failure states the following: You fail only when you can't accept failure.

How a person deals with personal failure determines, to a large degree, how successful that person will be. Everyone fails at one time or another, so it is essential to know how to respond appropriately.

Steve Largent, one of the greatest receivers in the history of the NFL, gives the following advice on how you can properly cope with failure. It is in the form of an acronym. (*Note*: Have the students complete the acronym on their worksheet.)

Forget about your failures. Don't dwell on past mistakes.

Anticipate failure. Realize that all people make mistakes.

Intensity is essential to everything you do. Never be a failure for lack of effort.

Learn from your mistakes. Don't repeat previous errors.

Understand why you failed. Diagnose your mistakes so as not to repeat them.

Respond; don't repeat errors. Responding corrects mistakes; reacting magnifies them.

Elevate your self-concept. It is okay to fail; everyone does. Now how are you going to deal with failure?

DO: (15 MINUTES)

* Lead a discussion covering the questions on the worksheet.
* Review the word of the day. Ask a student to use it correctly in a sentence.

Photo Credit: Stephen Dunn/Getty Images Sport

DO YOU HAVE THE CHARACTER TO HANDLE ADVERSITY?—WORKSHEET

"Affliction comes to us, not to make us sad but sober, not to make us sorry but wise."
—Henry Ward Beecher

F _____

A _____

I _____

L _____

U _____

R _____

E _____

For discussion:

1. What does the following statement mean: "How a person deals with personal failure determines, to a large degree, how successful that person will be."

   _____

   _____

2. Looking at the above acronym, choose one letter or aspect of failure that you need to work on. List some specific steps you can take to begin to improve that area.

   _____

   _____

3. Think of an adversity someone you admire has overcome. What can you learn from their response?

   _____

   _____

Word of the Day: Affliction—a cause of pain or distress

DO YOU HAVE THE CHARACTER TO HANDLE SUCCESS?—COACH'S NOTES

SAY: (5 MINUTES)

"The human race has had long experience and a fine tradition in surviving adversity. But we now face a task for which we have little experience—the task of surviving prosperity."

—Alan Greg, Educator

"When everything's going well, it is only natural that you just ride the crest and don't worry about anything. The Lord tried to get through to me by saying that I'd better get off my butt."

—Steve Bartkowski, NFL Quarterback

While success is something that every athlete wants, it creates an entirely new set of pressures and problems. Not every athlete who achieves success handles it well.

With success comes a temptation to slack off, to relax. That temptation is called complacency, which is a continuous struggle that all people have to fight. You constantly have to work on getting tougher on yourself.

The most important thing to do after winning is to get back to work. Winning can have a negative influence if you become too satisfied or complacent with your performance. Even in victory, be critical and look for mistakes you might have made. Why? To avoid them next time. Never be completely satisfied; keep searching for ways to improve. Always give a total effort. Pride in yourself and your ability comes through knowledge and hard work. Self-discipline is the key to harnessing the energy and dedication necessary to succeed.

When you think that you have mastered it all, humble yourself with the thought that learning is a lifetime process. The margin between a winner and a champion is only a little extra work.

The biggest danger probably comes when you are successful. You begin to think that you can get by without adequate preparation. You must get tougher on yourself as you become successful. It is so easy to let little things slip by if you are getting the desired results. You must constantly ask yourself, "Am I doing things correctly?" "Am I strong enough to handle success?"

Adolph Rupp once remarked, "Unfortunately, the road to anywhere is filled with many pitfalls and it takes a man of determination and character not to fall into them. As I have said many times, whenever you get your head above the average, someone will be there to take a poke at you. That is to be expected in any phase of life. However, as I have also said many times before, if you see a man on top of a mountain, he didn't just light there! Chances are he had to climb through many difficulties with a great expenditure of energy in order to get there, and the same is true of a man in any profession, be he a great attorney, a great minister, a great man of medicine, or a great businessman. I am certain he worked with a definite plan and an aim and purpose in life and will be envied by those less successful. I have always thought that the following little verse contained a good philosophy for everyone:

By your own soul learn to live,
And if men thwart you, take no heed,
If men hate you, have no care;
Sing your song, dream your dream,
Hope your hope, and pray your prayer.

"I am sure that if a person will follow this philosophy of life, he will be successful. To sit by and worry about criticism, which too often comes from the misinformed or from those incapable of passing judgment on an individual or a problem, is a waste of time."

DO: (15 MINUTES)

- Lead a discussion covering the questions on the worksheet.
- Review the word of the day. Ask a student to use it correctly in a sentence.

Photo Credit: Scott Barbour/Getty Images Sport

DO YOU HAVE THE CHARACTER TO HANDLE SUCCESS?—WORKSHEET

"To be on the alert is to live; to be lulled into security is to die."

—Oscar Wilde

For discussion:

1. "Probably the biggest danger comes when you are successful." Do you believe this statement is true? Why or why not?

_____

_____

_____

_____

_____

_____

2. List some specific things that you can do to handle success.

_____

_____

_____

_____

_____

_____

_____

Word of the Day: Complacency—self-satisfaction accompanied by a lack of awareness of actual deficiencies

DO YOU HAVE THE CHARACTER TO HANDLE CRITICS?—COACH'S NOTES

SAY: (5 MINUTES)

Criticism can be easily avoided—if you say nothing, do nothing, and become nothing. Mediocre people play it safe and avoid criticism at all costs. Champions, however, risk criticism every time they perform. The more you do in life and the more you accomplish, the more you risk being criticized.

However, it is important to remember that it's not the critic who counts. Theodore Roosevelt put it this way: "It is not the critic who counts, not the man who points out how the strong man stumbles or where the doer of deeds could have done them better. The credit belongs to the man who is actually in the arena, whose face is marred by dust and sweat and blood, who strives valiantly, who errs and comes short again and again because there is no effort without error and shortcomings, who knows the great devotion, who spends himself in a worthy cause, who at the best knows in the end the high achievement of triumph and who at worst, if he fails while daring greatly, knows his place shall never be with those timid and cold souls who know neither victory nor defeat."

If you are successful, people will be jealous and criticize you. Don't let that distract you from reaching your goal. It is easy to criticize other people, but it is hard to duplicate their efforts. Critics are not the leaders or doers in life. The leaders and doers are too busy with their own accomplishments to criticize.

It takes a belief in yourself to overcome the fear of criticism. Belief is the knowledge that you can do something. It is the inner feeling that what you undertake, you can accomplish. One of life's greatest fears is criticism. Some people never participate in competitive sports for the simple reason that they are afraid of being criticized. "Nothing ventured, nothing failed" would be their reinterpretation of an old saying. This fear of criticism is more than just a lack of confidence. It is a preoccupation with self-image designed to minimize experiences of defeat.

Athletics, if they are to provide lessons in life, must always be accompanied by the possibility of criticism. To be criticized in athletics is to realize an area of weakness, not to succumb to it. It appears at times as though some people are looking for a reason to quit. Upon noticing a glaring weakness and experiencing criticism, an athlete may just "check out" of the situation and leave it alone forever. It seems so easy to forsake a real test, but a pattern of response could be developed that would prove very unfulfilling throughout life. Criticism must be looked at as a challenge to overcome.

However, it is true that some weaknesses are inherent. For these so-called weaknesses, everyone has strengths that can be used to compensate. For every inherent weakness, a corresponding strength exists. Infielders whose arms are not necessarily strong can compensate with a quick release of the ball or greater use of their bodies. The pitcher who can't throw the "heater" can compensate by changing speeds and keeping the batter off-stride.

Don't be hurt, be not surprised,
If what you do is criticized.
There is always one or more who can
Find fault with anything you plan.
Mistakes are made, we can't deny,
But only made by those who try.

Eleanor Roosevelt once said that, "No one can make you feel inferior without your permission." It is up to you to refuse to give that permission to anyone.

Former NFL quarterback Brian Sipe refused to give that permission when he said, "The criticism about my size and my arm doesn't bother me because I know I can compensate inside myself for any physical shortcomings I may have. When the going gets tough, I know I can gut it out."

DO: (15 MINUTES)

- Lead a discussion of the questions on the worksheet.
- Review the word of the day. Ask a student to use it correctly in a sentence.

DO YOU HAVE THE CHARACTER TO HANDLE CRITICS?—WORKSHEET

"Courage is resistance to fear, master of fear—not absence of fear."

—Mark Twain

For discussion:

1. How do you react when you are criticized…

   in front of others? _____

   _____

   by a parent? _____

   _____

   unfairly? _____

   _____

   for outperforming others (in academics or athletics)? _____

   _____

2. How do you give others permission to make you feel inferior (e.g., by accepting their negative comments as true)?

   _____

   _____

   _____

   _____

   _____

Word of the Day: Courage—ability to conquer fear or despair

DO YOU HAVE THE CHARACTER TO ACCEPT RESPONSIBILITY?—COACH'S NOTES

LESSON #4

SAY: (5 MINUTES)

The day you take complete responsibility for yourself, the day you stop making excuses, that is the day you head to the top! The power to fulfill your dreams is within each of you. You alone have the responsibility to shape your life. When you understand this, you will know that nothing and no one can deny you success. You are the one pushing yourself forward or holding yourself back. The power to succeed or fail is yours alone.

Accept responsibility for yourself. If you are wrong, admit it, take the blame, and get on with it. Do not dwell on the past. You can only change the present. Remember, it is not what happens to you that counts in life, it is how you take it and what you make of it.

The *Bible* says: "As ye sow, so also shall ye reap." The Chinese have the saying, "If a man plants melons, he will reap melons; if he sows beans, he will reap beans." Good begets good, and evil leads to evil. This statement is one of the eternal, fundamental truths of the universe—the law of cause and effect.

What the statement means is that for every cause, a consequence occurs that is nearly equal in intensity. If you make good use of your mind, skills, and talents, it will result in positive rewards in your life. And if you take the personal responsibility to make the best use of your natural talents in the time you have, the effect will be an enormous gain in personal happiness and success.

Success on any major scale requires you to accept responsibility. In the final analysis, the individual person is responsible for living his own life. If he persists in shifting this responsibility to someone else, he will never grow as a person.

The men and women of West Point have a motto: "No excuses, Sir!" When you make a mistake or fail at an assignment, avoid whining, making excuses, or blaming others. Accept a failure as a part of your learning process. Successful people live up to a mistake as simply and easily as they accept praise. Plan and prepare a way to do better next time.

Responsibility liberates you as an individual. It means making the best of what you have with your mind, talents, skills, and abilities. Taking responsibility gives you the power to control the direction and outcome of your life. You are responsible for you!

The following is the personal philosophy of Henry Bartell Zachry, a man who understood what it meant to take responsibility: "I do not choose to be a common man. It is my right to be uncommon if I can. I seek opportunity, not security. I will refuse to be a kept citizen, to be humbled and dulled by having my state and nation look after me. I want to dream and to build, to fail and to succeed and never to be numbered among those weak, timid souls who have known neither victory nor defeat. I know that happiness can come only from the inside through hard, constructive work and sincere, positive thinking. I know that the so-called pleasures of the moment should not be confused with a state of happiness. I know that I can get a measure of inner-satisfaction from any job if I intelligently plan and courageously execute it. I know that if I put forth every iota of strength that I possess—physical, mental, spiritual—toward the accomplishment of a worthwhile task ere I fall exhausted by the wayside, the unseen hand, will reach out and pull me through. Yes, I want to live dangerously, plan my procedures on the basis of calculated risks, to resolve the problems of everyday living into a measure of inner peace. I know if I know how to do all this, I will know how to live and, if I know how to live, I will know how to die."

Do you have the character to accept the responsibility for your own life?

DO: (15 MINUTES)

* Give the students at least 10 minutes to think about and begin to write their answers to Question #1. Encourage them to take this assignment seriously. Those who do will probably not finish this question in one sitting. They will need to take several days to think and re-read what they have written.
* Lead a discussion of Question #2 on the worksheet.
* Review the word of the day. Ask a student to use it correctly in a sentence.

DO YOU HAVE THE CHARACTER TO ACCEPT RESPONSIBILITY?—WORKSHEET

"I believe that every right implies a responsibility; every opportunity, an obligation; every possession, a duty."

—John D. Rockerfeller

For discussion:

1. Take some time and write your own personal philosophy of life. How do you want to live your life? What are the qualities you hope people see in you?

_____

_____

_____

_____

_____

_____

2. What is one action step you can take today to show that you am responsible for your life (e.g., admit a mistake, get you homework done without anyone telling you to do so)?

_____

_____

_____

_____

_____

_____

Word of the Day: Hypocrisy—pretending to have qualities that one does not, especially moral superiority

NEVER, NEVER, NEVER QUIT—COACH'S NOTES

LESSON #5

SAY: (5 MINUTES)

"Our greatest weakness lies in giving up. The most certain way to succeed is to always try just one more time."

—Thomas Edison

"Never give in. Never, never, never, never! Never yield in any way great or small, except to convictions of honor and good sense. Never yield to force and the apparently overwhelming might of the enemy."

—Winston Churchill

No team or individual has ever achieved greatness without, somewhere along the way, facing and overcoming a great obstacle. The ability to overcome is a trait that only belongs to a champion. As an obstacle lies in front of you, you are either going to overcome or quit. Champions are not born of people who always have things go their way. Winners are not those who go through a season and never face a real challenge. Usually, when a team is down, someone comes along with a play, an effort, or an attitude to light the fire.

No matter what happens in business, life, or in sports, don't quit. Quitters are losers; they have the bad habit of giving up before it is over. Winners set goals and work hard; they do not let anything stop them from reaching their goal. The only true way to fail to reach your goal is to quit. It makes sense that the more time and effort you invest in preparation, the more you will want to win. Why? Because you have more of yourself invested in the process. When you make a strong investment you develop a habit of winning, because you will do everything possible not to lose or quit. It is hard to surrender when you have a lot invested.

Not quitting sounds easy, but it is not. If you are not in condition or have not sacrificed, it will be easier for you to quit. If you have not made the great investments of time and effort, it will be easier for you to quit. It is logical that the more you commit yourself to what you are doing, the harder it will be for you to give up. Very few reap the really great returns because very few are willing to make the really big investments.

Winners have a strong mental attitude that refuses to let them give up. Some people call this "heart." But times will arise when you lose—even the great champions do on occasion. When you lose, lose with pride and in style. Go down swinging. Take your best shot and don't quit! The following poem reinforces that spirit.

Don't Quit

When things go wrong, as they sometimes will,
When the road you're trudging seems all uphill,
When the funds are low and the debts are high,
And you want to smile, but you have to sigh,
When care is pressing you down a bit—
Rest if you must, but don't you quit.

Life is queer with its twists and turns,
As every one of us sometimes learns,
And many a person turns about
When they might have won had they stuck it out.
Don't give up though the pace seems slow—
You may succeed with another blow.

Often the struggler has given up
When he might have captured the victor's cup;
And he learned too late when the night came down,
How close he was to the golden crown.
So stick to the fight when you're hardest hit,
It's when things seem worst that you mustn't quit.

DO: (15 MINUTES)

- Lead a discussion covering the questions on the student worksheet.
- Review the word of the day. Ask a student to use it correctly in a sentence.

LESSON #5

NEVER, NEVER, NEVER QUIT—WORKSHEET

"Loyalty means nothing unless it has at its heart the absolute principle of self-sacrifice."

—Woodrow Wilson

For discussion:

1. Give an example of an experience in your life (or in the life of someone you know) where you succeeded because you overcame a tough situation.

   _____

   _____

   _____

2. Give an example of an experience in your life (or in the life of someone you know) where you failed to reach your goal because you quit.

   _____

   _____

   _____

3. Why is it hard to persist when the going gets tough?

   _____

   _____

   _____

4. How can you overcome one of the obstacles listed in Question #3?

   _____

   _____

   _____

Word of the Day: Loyalty—faithfulness to a country, cause, or friend

LESSONS FOR A LIFETIME—COACH'S NOTES

SAY: (5 MINUTES)

At this moment, you are in one of the most exciting phases of your life—your youth. The whole world lies before you. The opportunities are limitless. What you do, where you go, and what you become depends on your willingness to work toward a goal. As an athlete, you have already learned the virtue of perseverance. You have learned that you can overcome obstacles with the proper effort and practice. If you pursue other goals throughout life with the same tenacity, you will succeed. Most importantly, the real key to success is within yourself. No one can give it to you or take it from you. You hold your destiny in your hands.

Unless a man believes in himself and makes a total commitment to his career and puts everything he has into it—his mind, his body, and his heart—what is life worth to him? Intensity of effort is the difference between success and failure, not only in sports, but in life.

In sports, that intensity is so closely related to winning that competitors are generally quick to accept it as a basic quality of their play. It enables the shorter player to out-jump the bigger one, the slower player to out-quick the faster one, and the player of lesser ability to finish ahead of the more skilled performer. The same intensity of effort is absolutely essential in the game of life as well. It is the difference between success and failure.

It has been often said that athletics challenge the body, mind, and spirit. The values of leadership, sacrifice, and discipline, which are acquired through athletics, have served as useful tools for many. The combination of classroom academics and participation in extracurricular activities adds up to a well-rounded young adult. The values that make you a good athlete and good student are the same values that will help you throughout your entire life, no matter what you do.

A young person's involvement in athletics holds a tremendous potential for development and learning. Participation in athletics has the potential to teach self-discipline, cooperation, sacrifice, and countless other valuable character qualities. In a world where mediocrity is the mode, no greater challenge exists than giving your best in whatever you do. Vince Lombardi said that a man's finest hour is when he works his heart out for a good cause and lies exhausted on the field of battle, victorious. In the Bible, Paul implores the Corinthians to "run your race to win." In other words, give your best shot in everything you do. Those students who give their best in school, and those athletes who always work at practice, become the successful citizens of tomorrow.

Consider what Bob Lilly, a former defensive tackle for the NFL, once stated about the principles you have been learning:

"After reviewing my athletic career, spiced with five years' experience of operating my own business, I can offer the following guidelines to achieving success in both sports and the business world, because the same principles apply.

"First of all, you need to have both long-range goals and short-range goals. In my case, the long-range goal was to play pro football. But in order to do this, I had to have short-range goals such as increasing agility, putting on weight, building strength, and being competitive enough to get a college scholarship. In college I had the same basic goals, along with the development of self-discipline and making my grades. After attaining my goal of becoming a professional ball player, I set new goals—becoming an All-Pro and winning the Super Bowl.

"The next ingredient in my formula for success is dedication. This includes rigorous self-discipline, consistent hard work, and maintenance of a strict routine. With the right attitude of dedication, you can make every day profitable toward achieving the big goal.

"Of course, to be successful, one must have good ability which is God-given. Our Creator designs each of us with specific talents, but then we have the choice to develop our potential or not. A winner will choose to make the most of his assets and even overcompensate for areas of weakness.

"To be successful, one must have experience. In my case, I played in five unsuccessful seasons with the Cowboys before finally starting to win. Each losing season gave me some valuable experience that finally contributed to the winning seasons.

"The final attribute I wish to list for a winner is that of self-confidence. There is a saying: 'A chain is only as strong as its weakest link.' Lack of confidence could be the weak link in the chain, so one must believe in oneself in order to achieve success. Self-confidence comes from learning your own strengths and weaknesses. Through much experience in competing one arrives at this knowledge. Then one can build up weak areas and focus on the strong ones."

What you are learning during your school years—not only in the classroom, but also on the playing field—truly are lessons that will be with you for a lifetime.

DO: (15 MINUTES)

- Let the students complete Question #1 individually. Divide the team into groups to work on the list for Question #2.
- Share the lists so that everyone in the room has a complete list of words. Try to come up with a list of at least 15 qualities that successful people possess. Steer the groups past such things as money and fame to focus on the character traits listed in the lesson.
- Have people share their acronyms from Question #3. If someone has a two- or three-letter name, have them use their middle or last name.
- Review the word of the day and ask a student to use it correctly in a sentence.

LESSONS FOR A LIFETIME—WORKSHEET

"There is no expedient to which a man will not go to avoid the labor of thinking."
—Thomas Edison

LESSON #6

For discussion:

1. Write down the names of three people you know or historical figures who you believe to be successful.

    _____

    _____

    _____

    _____

2. List some character traits or qualities of the people listed in Question #1 (e.g., honest, knowledgeable, dependable).

    _____

    _____

    _____

    _____

    _____

3. Using the letters of your name, form an acronym that describes your character. You may use qualities listed in Question #1 or any other accurate, positive, descriptive words.

    For example, "Terry" could be:
    Talented
    Enthusiastic
    Realistic
    Responsible
    Yearns for knowledge

Word of the Day: Expedient—immediately advantageous without regard for ethics or principles

LESSON #7

A COMMITMENT TO EXCELLENCE—COACH'S NOTES

SAY: (5 MINUTES)

People often have so much of everything that it is difficult to encourage a young athlete to sacrifice. When the going gets rough and the body and mind begin to experience pain and anguish, a less demanding alternative always seem to be available. To "stay with" a thing sometimes requires the sacrifice of personal comfort and feelings; it requires a commitment to excellence. The greatest benefit of success is not recognition received, but the investment made and the satisfaction gained from previous sacrifices. Through sacrifice and a commitment to excellence, character is developed and character wins more games than any other single trait an athlete may possess.

Athletes are born with varying degrees of natural ability. Sacrifice and a commitment to excellence are required to develop that ability. Time, hard work, continuous practice, and repetition all go into the making of a good athlete.

You can be as great as you want to be. If you believe in yourself and have the courage, determination, dedication, and competitive drive, and if you are willing to give up the little things in life to accomplish an ultimate goal down the road, it can be done.

To be a true winner, you must make a commitment to excellence in your sport and in your life. This type of commitment means being willing to do whatever is necessary to become successful. You must be willing to work hard and push yourself physically until it hurts. Any player who walks off the field or court after playing a full game and is not physically spent has not worked to his physical potential.

To be a winner you must be willing to make sacrifices, including maintaining good training habits, getting the proper amount of rest, and eating a balanced diet. If you have a true commitment to excellence, you will give up anything that does not help you become better as an athlete or a person. Don't be content with mediocrity—strive to live up to the greatness within you.

The renowned football coach Vince Lombardi once made the following observation about making a commitment to excellence:

"I owe almost everything to football, in which I have spent the greater part of my life, and I have never lost my respect, my admiration, nor my love for what I consider a great game. Each Sunday after the battle, one group savors victory, another group wallows in the bitterness of defeat. The many hurts seem a small price to pay for having won, and there is no reason at all which compensates for having lost.

"For the winner there is 100 percent elation, 100 percent laughter, 100 percent fun, and for the loser the only thing left is a 100 percent resolution and 100 percent determination. The game, I think, is a great deal like life. Every man makes his own personal commitment toward excellence and toward victory. Although you know ultimate victory can never be completely won, it must be pursued with all of one's might and each week there is a new encounter, each year a new challenge.

"All of the rings and all of the money and all of the color and all of the display, they linger only in a memory. But the spirit, the will to win, the will to excel, these are the things that endure and these are the qualities, of course, that are so much more important than any of the events that occur.

"I'd like to say that the quality of any man's life is a full measure of that man's personal commitment to excellence and to victory, regardless of what field he may be in."

DO: (15 MINUTES)

- Lead a discussion covering the questions found on the student worksheet.
- Review the word of the day. Ask a student to use it correctly in a sentence.

Photo Credit: Stephen Dunn/Getty Images Sport

A COMMITMENT TO EXCELLENCE—WORKSHEET

"Prudence is an attitude that keeps life safe, but does not often make it happy."
—Samuel Johnson

For discussion:

1. "Desire is the ingredient that enables a person with average ability to successfully compete with those who have far more—by using more of the ability the person possesses." Discuss this statement. Give an example of an experience in your life or in the life of someone you know when you used your average abilities to succeed.

   _____

   _____

   _____

   _____

2. Working as a group, discuss the following statements and decide which one is most meaningful and why.

   • Failure has been correctly identified as "the line of lease persistence."

   • Doing the tough things today will prepare us for the big things tomorrow.

   • Ability is important—dependability is critical.

   _____

   _____

   _____

   _____

   _____

Word of the Day: Prudence—careful management; discreet or cautious behavior

CLASS—COACH'S NOTES

SAY: (5 MINUTES)

What is "class"? Over the years several people have defined it in some different terms. For example, John Wooden once said that, "Class is an intangible quality which commands, rather than demands, the respect of others. This is because those who have it are truly considerate of others, are courteous and polite without being subservient, are not disagreeable when they disagree, are good listeners, and are at peace with themselves because they do not knowingly do wrong. In short, a person with class might well be defined as one who practices 'The Golden Rule' in both his professional and personal life."

Roger Staubach, on the other hand, observed that class is, "Striving hard to be the best at what you do while taking the needs of others into consideration." Viewing it differently, Jack Nicklaus remarked that, "Class is being honest—both with others and with yourself. Class is treating others as you would like them to treat you." In turn, Ara Parseghian stated that, "Class is a quality that others admire because its behavior can be counted on as natural, simplistic, consistent, humane, and of the highest standard in all human relationships; it stands the test of time."

Anything in life or in athletics can be done in two ways—with class or without class. It doesn't cost any more or take any extra time or energy to have class. Having class does not make you any less a competitor or any less aggressive as an athlete. You do not lose any advantage by having class. As a matter of fact, you gain an advantage.

How does class give you an advantage over your opponent? Simply stated, you will have the poise that allows you to concentrate better, which helps you perform better. You will have the respect and admiration of your opponents and the fans. People tend to pull for athletes who show "class."

What exactly is class? It is one of those valuable, "intangible" personal traits that is in high demand because it is so rare. Many people, unfortunately, do not have it. Having class means being a good person, showing good sportsmanship, always taking responsibility for the consequences of your actions, and being considerate to others. You always have class if you show pride, have humility and poise, and display self-confidence without being arrogant.

Athletes with class handle victory and defeat in the same way, with their heads held high. They do not brag in victory or make excuses in defeat. They always praise their opponent for a job well done and they admit their mistakes. Class is also honesty. Honesty with yourself makes you comfortable with yourself. Being honest with yourself also makes you understand that you are no better or worse than anyone else. Class is good manners, cleanliness (of the body and mind), consideration for others, and an appropriate degree of humility.

Class is also an intangible thing. Different people show it in different ways, but it does not take long to surface and it's easily recognizable. Class always shows itself, whether you win or lose. People can tell instantly if you have class by watching you perform and interact with others. Fame, fortune, trophies, and glory are all fine, but they alone will not give you class. Only you can give yourself class.

Consider the following hallmarks of class:

- Class never runs scared. It is sure-footed and confident in the knowledge that you can meet life head-on and handle whatever comes along.
- Class never makes excuses. It takes its lumps and learns from past mistakes.
- Class is considerate of others. It knows that good manners are nothing more than a series of petty sacrifices.
- Class never tries to build itself up by tearing others down.
- Class is already up and does not need to strive to look better by making others look worse.
- Class can "walk with kings and keep its virtue, and talk with crowds and keep the common touch." Everyone is comfortable with a person who has class—because he is comfortable with himself.

If you have class, you don't need much of anything else. If you don't have it, whatever else you have just doesn't make much difference.

DO: (15 MINUTES)

- Discuss the questions found on the worksheet.
- Review the word of the day. Ask a student to use it correctly in a sentence.

Photo Credit: Getty Images/Getty Images Sport

CLASS—WORKSHEET

"We know next to nothing about virtually everything. It is not necessary to know the origin of the universe; it is necessary to want to know. Civilization depends not on any particular knowledge, but on the disposition to crave knowledge."

—George F. Will

For discussion:

1. In your own words, define "class."

_____

_____

_____

_____

2. Do you believe "class" is an important character trait for an athlete to possess? Why or why not?

_____

_____

_____

_____

3. List someone you know who exhibits class. Today, let this person be your role model. Ask yourself, "How would he or she respond with class to this situation?"

_____

_____

_____

_____

Word of the Day: Inquisitive—curious; inquiring; probing

THE "MIRROR" TEST—COACH'S NOTES

LESSON #9

SAY: (5 MINUTES)

John McKay, a college football coach, once made the following observation about the mirror test: "I am a big believer in the mirror test. By that I mean that you should not worry about the fans or the press or trying to satisfy the expectations of anyone else. All that matters is if you can look in the mirror and honestly tell the person you see there that you have done your best." That thought is also expressed in the following poem:

The Man in the Glass

When you get what you want in your struggle for self
And the world makes you king for a day.
Just go to the mirror and look at yourself
And see what that man has to say.

For it isn't your father or mother or wife
Whose judgment upon you must pass.
The fellow whose verdict counts most in your life
Is the one staring back from the glass.

You may be like Jack Horner and chisel a plum
And think you're a wonderful guy.
But the man in the glass says you're only a bum
If you can't look him straight in the eye.

He's the fellow to please—never mind all the rest,
For he's with you clear to the end.
And you've passed your most dangerous, difficult test
If the man in the glass is your friend.

You may fool the whole world down the pathway of years
And get pats on the back as you pass.
But your final reward will be heartache and tears
If you've cheated the man in the glass.

Once you begin to develop your character, you must make an honest self-evaluation, which can be difficult. Look in the mirror and ask yourself, "What do I see?" You can fool others—your coaches, teammates, as well as your family and friends—but you can't fool yourself. Being honest with yourself is a big step in growing up.

Every athlete should seriously consider the job he has done after every practice or every game. He should go into the locker room and look into a mirror and ask himself one question: "Did I do the very best possible job I could do?" If the answer is "yes," he has done his work well. However, if he has doubts—if he says to himself, "If only I had tried a little harder, I would have made that tackle," or, "If I had only given a little extra effort, I could have intercepted that pass"—then he has not done his job.

John Wooden's college basketball record at UCLA is one of the most impressive in sports history. During a 12-year span, his Bruins won 10 NCAA basketball championships. With that record, you know his teams were consistently doing the things that they could do best. His message to his players was to focus on what they could do, and not to worry about what they could not do.

Do not waste time or energy worrying about whether you are going to win or lose. Concentrate on preparing yourself to become the very best athlete you can be—both mentally and physically. Strive to gain an advantage over your opponent in every possible manner—in strength, technique, conditioning, and mental toughness. You will feel so confident that you expect to win, and that is the biggest part of winning.

After each game or practice, ask yourself if you have given 100 percent, which is a very high standard that is seldom, if ever, reached. Don't fool yourself. No one is perfect. The only real losers in life, and in sports, are those who refuse to admit their faults.

You must recognize your weaknesses before you can even begin to think about correcting them. Find out where you made a mistake to determine where you need help. If you lie to yourself or are not open-minded enough to admit that what you are doing is wrong, you will never correct it.

Nothing comes easy in life, but if you believe in yourself, are honest in your self-appraisal, are able to take constructive criticism, and are prepared to give 100 percent total effort in everything you do, you will always be able to hold your head high.

Each of you must work to make the best of your natural ability. You have to do the things that you know to be right rather than those that make you look good or make you popular. When all is said and done, when you put your head on the pillow at the end of the day, it is just you and God—and you cannot fool either one.

DO: (15 MINUTES)

- Lead a discussion covering the questions on the student worksheet. You may not want the students to answer Question #3 aloud.
- Review the word of the day. Ask a student to use it correctly in a sentence.

THE "MIRROR" TEST—WORKSHEET

"Life is a mirror and will reflect back on the thinker what he thinks into it."

—Ernest Holmes

For discussion:

1. What is the most important lesson you learned from the poem, "The Man in the Glass"?

    _____

    _____

    _____

2. Developing character includes making an honest self-evaluation. Write two weaknesses you have in each of the three areas listed.

    Athletics: _____

    _____

    Academics: _____

    _____

    Relationships: _____

    _____

3. During the time you have spent in athletics, what has been one memorable character-developing experience for you?

    _____

    _____

    _____

Word of the Day: Ambiguous—capable of having more than one interpretation

STAND FOR SOMETHING—COACH'S NOTES

SAY: (5 MINUTES)

It is often difficult, especially for young people facing tremendous peer pressure, to stand up for what you believe and perhaps go against the grain. However, to be successful in life, you must not succumb to these pressures, but instead have the courage it takes to stand by your convictions.

Establish solid principles and standards to live by and do so early in life. It is so important to build a solid foundation for yourself when you are young, so that you may build upon it throughout your entire life.

Keep a firm hold over your own life at all times and learn not to follow negative influences. Be a leader over your own self! Have the courage to stand on your principles. Do not quest for popularity at the expense of morality, ethics, and honesty. Daniel Webster taught that what is popular is not always right, and what is right is not always popular. Do not be afraid to speak up. Do not be afraid to take a stand. You cannot make any useful contribution to society unless you do.

Thomas Jefferson summed up his philosophy of life this way: "In matters of principle, stand like a rock; in matters of taste, swim with the current. Give up money, give up fame, give up science, give up the earth itself and all it contains, rather than do an immoral act. And never suppose that in any possible situation or under any circumstances, it is best for you to do a dishonorable thing. Whenever you are to do a thing, though it can never be known but to yourself, ask yourself how you would act were all the world looking at you, and act accordingly. He who permits himself to tell a lie once finds it much easier to do it a second and third time, till at length it becomes habitual; he tells a lie without attending to it, and truths without the world believing him." You could learn a great lesson from Thomas Jefferson if you make his philosophy your own.

Be your own person! If you do not want to drink, do not drink. If you do not want to smoke, do not smoke. The same goes for using drugs, lying, cheating, and other negative things. Make your decision now. Will drugs, alcohol, and cigarettes help you in reaching your goals in athletics or in life? The answer is a simple "no." They can only do you great harm, so eliminate them from your life.

You must have the courage of your convictions. Follow your commitment to excellence and avoid anything that stands in your way. If you do not, you are only fooling and hurting yourself.

Associate with people of good qualities; it is better to be alone than in bad company. If your friends have lower standards than you do, pull them up to your level. Do not drop down to theirs.

Have the courage to take a stand. Dare to be different. Dare to be great! In that regard, Joe Paterno once remarked, "We need people who influence their peers and who cannot be detoured from their convictions by peers who do not have any convictions."

The following poem was originally written about a father. However, as athletes, younger kids are looking up to you as their example, so the message of the poem is still applicable to each of you.

Little Eyes Upon You

There are little eyes upon you and they're watching night and day.
There are little ears that quickly take in every word you say.
There are little hands all eager to do anything you do;
And a little boy who is dreaming of the day he'll be like you.

You're the little fellow's idol, you're the wisest of the wise.
In his little mind about you no suspicions ever rise.
He believes in you devoutly, holds all that you say and do;
He will say and do, in your way, when he's grown up like you.

There's a wide eyed little fellow who believes you're always right;
And his eyes are always opened, and he watches day and night.
You are setting an example every day in all you do,
For the little boy who's waiting to grow up to be like you.

DO: (15 MINUTES)

- Lead a discussion covering the questions on the student worksheet.
- Review the word of the day. Ask a student to use it correctly in a sentence.

STAND FOR SOMETHING—WORKSHEET

"You can't hold a man down without staying down on him."
—Booker T. Washington

For discussion:

1. Having character means being your own person. List five standards in your life that you will not compromise (e.g., I will not smoke).

_____

_____

_____

_____

2. List three positive influences your friends have on you.

_____

_____

_____

3. List any negative influences your friends have on you? What can you do to stand strong against those influences?

_____

_____

_____

4. Is there something you need to change in your life to be a better example to younger athletes who are watching you?

_____

_____

_____

Word of the Day: Ambition—eager desire for success or power

TOUGH LOVE—COACH'S NOTES

LESSON #11

SAY: (5 MINUTES)

Nothing is more beneficial than tough love. Tough love is the love that usually goes along with doing something that you don't want to do, but that you must do because you love someone. Some parents may tell their children before they spank them that the spanking will hurt them more than it hurts the child. It hurts in a totally different way, but the pain of tough love, of disciplining someone you love, is very real and it is perhaps the most difficult task a parent must do. The following story illustrates what tough love is and what it can do.

A boy with cerebral palsy was forced at a very young age to wear braces on his legs every night while he slept. His parents' desire was for their child to have a chance in life. This desire was translated into the actions they took so that he could have that chance. Some of those actions were tough, really tough, because they involved a special kind of love that was so deep that it demanded they overrule their natural sympathy and compassion. Every night, the parents had to put special braces on the boy's legs. Many times, when the parents forced those braces tighter according to the doctor's instructions, the young boy would cry and plead with them to ease up or leave them off for "just one night." The parents would have given almost anything to comply, but their love was so deep that they said "no" to the boy's tears for the moment, which meant they were saying "yes" to his health and happiness for a lifetime. That love was tough love. Because of that tough love, the young boy was able to live a normal life and become a successful businessman, husband, and father.

Sometimes, the toughest act to do is to love someone so much that you do not allow them to accept less than the best. Often the recipient of tough love does not realize what is being done for them until much later. One of the reasons it is so difficult is that, when you give tough love, you usually are not appreciated immediately and you have to be willing to know the rewards will come in the future. If the rewards will not come for you, they will certainly come for the one you love.

The best teachers and coaches are the ones who understand tough love. These educators often are not the most popular while the students are in school, but they are the teachers that the students come back and thank when they get out on their own.

Tough love is doing what is best for the person regardless of sympathy or compassion. Do you love someone enough to do what is best for him or her? That is the question.

DO: (15 MINUTES)

- Lead a discussion from the questions on the student worksheet. Be sure to let the students do the talking and always ask for specific examples.
- Review the word of the day. Ask a student to use it correctly in a sentence.

TOUGH LOVE—WORKSHEET

"No one would have crossed the ocean if he could have gotten off the ship in the storm."

—Charles Kettering

For discussion:

1. How was tightening the braces an act of tough love?

_____

_____

_____

_____

2. What was the easy choice to make?

_____

_____

_____

3. Do you ever have to "tighten the braces" of your friends? Can you give an example?

_____

_____

_____

4. What do you think of when you think of tough love? Why?

_____

_____

_____

Word of the Day: Compassion—consciousness of other's distress together with a desire to alleviate it

THE REAL TEST OF FRIENDSHIP—COACH'S NOTES

LESSON #12

SAY: (5 MINUTES)

The following story does a good job of illustrating what is meant by friendship. This powerful story is about a deep friendship between two soldiers in the trenches of World War I.

Two buddies were serving together in the mud and misery of the European stalemate. Month after month they lived out their lives in the cold and the mud, under constant fire. From time to time, one side or the other would rise up out of the trenches, fling their bodies against the opposing line, and slink back to lick their wounds, bury their dead, and wait to do it all over again.

In the process, friendships were forged in the misery. Day after day, night after night, terror after terror, they talked of life and family, of hopes and what they would do if and when they ever returned home. On one more fruitless charge, Jim fell, severely wounded. Bill made it back to the relative safety of the trenches. Meanwhile, Jim lay suffering underneath the night flares, between the trenches, alone. The shelling continued, and the danger was at his feet; between the trenches was no place to be. Still, Bill wished to reach his friend to comfort him, to offer the encouragement that only friends can offer. The officer in charge refused to let Bill leave the trench. It was simply too dangerous. Once the officer turned his back, Bill went over the top. Ignoring the concussion of the incoming rounds and the pounding in his chest, he made it to Jim.

Sometime later he managed to get Jim back to the safety of the trenches. His friend had died shortly after he had gotten to him. The somewhat self-righteous officer, seeing Jim's body, cynically asked Bill if it had been worth the risk. Bill's response was without hesitation, "Yes, Sir, it was. My friend's last words made it more than worth it. He looked up at me and said, 'I knew you'd come.'"

DO: (15 MINUTES)

- Lead a discussion from the questions on the student worksheet. Be sure to let the students do the talking and always ask for specific examples.
- Review the word of the day. Ask a student to use it correctly in a sentence.

THE REAL TEST OF FRIENDSHIP—WORKSHEET

"Blessed are they who have a gift of making friends, for it is one of God's best gifts. It involves many things, but above all, the power of going out of one's self, and appreciating whatever is noble and loving in another."

—Thomas Hughes

For discussion:

1. Give an example of when a friend has helped you through a tough time.

_____

_____

_____

_____

_____

_____

_____

_____

2. Give an example of a time when you were there for a friend.

_____

_____

_____

_____

_____

_____

_____

_____

Word of the Day: Selfless—having no concern for self; unselfish

LEADERSHIP

Photo Credit: Craig Jones/Getty Images Sport

Chapter 6

"Leadership is the ability to lift and inspire."

—Paul Dietze

LESSON #1

THE IMPORTANCE OF LEADERS AND LEADERSHIP TO THE TEAM—COACH'S NOTES

SAY: (5 MINUTES)

Leadership is the key ingredient needed for a championship-caliber team. As Lou Holtz observed, "Leadership is the most important factor in the development of a championship team."

The greatest need of your team in this or any other year is an abundance of good leaders. They are needed during the off-season and preseason training, as well as during the season. They are needed during the building and developing of individual skills, during the phase of putting these skills together to form a team, and during each game you play. However, the most important class is the seniors. For this team to be successful, the seniors must play the best of their careers.

Leadership is a skill that is possessed by all, but used by only a few. Leadership can be learned by anyone, taught to everyone, and denied to no one. Everyone has leadership potential.

One of the greatest contributions a player can make to a team is to become a good leader. Assuming a role as a leader is a most satisfying experience. An opportunity to be a leader is a privilege and a challenge. It should be approached with confidence, because nearly all players of good character, reasonable physical skills, and ambition can learn to be good leaders. The need for good leaders is great and the opportunities are unlimited.

Being a good leader involves no mysterious methods or profound philosophical approaches. It is all quite simple and reasonable. The young player expects and wants to do the right thing. Improper behavior generally springs from ignorance. If a player does something wrong, a good leader simply tells him or shows him how to do it right. This rule applies on and off the field, in and out of the classroom, and on and off the campus. Both the coaches and you as leaders of this squad must believe that all players mean to do the right thing until it is proven otherwise.

Success or failure of an athletic team will depend to a great extent on the kind of leadership displayed. Many average teams have become great through fine leadership. And many potentially great teams never developed because of poor leadership. A great team must have great leaders.

DO: (15 MINUTES)

- Lead the team through the discussion questions found on the worksheet. Guide all answers toward leadership. (For example, the answer to Question #1 should include the idea that the team needs an abundance of leadership.)
- Review the word of the day. Ask a student to use it correctly in a sentence.

THE IMPORTANCE OF LEADERS AND LEADERSHIP TO THE TEAM—WORKSHEET

"Leadership is a matter of having people look at you and gain confidence by seeing how you react. If you are in control, they are in control."

—Tom Landry

For discussion:

1. What is the greatest need of your team?

_____

_____

_____

2. Why must a team have an abundance of leaders?

_____

_____

3. Who on your team can be a leader?

_____

_____

4. What is one of the greatest contributions a player can make to the team?

_____

_____

5. A leader has been defined as one who knows the way, goes the way, and shows the way. What does that mean to you?

_____

_____

Word of the Day: Contribute—to play a significant part in bringing about an end or result

WHAT IS A LEADER?—COACH'S NOTES

SAY: (5 MINUTES)

Fill in the blanks in the definition of a leader on your worksheet. A leader is a person fitted by force of ideas, character, or by strength of will or administrative ability to arouse, incite, and direct people in conduct and achievement. Most importantly, a leader is someone who can lead himself. Consider the following definition concerning *what is meant by "force of ideas"* in detail: Force of ideas refers to having strong thoughts, thinking thoughts of excellence, and having a strong, positive approach. A great leader possesses this type of thinking.

All great teachers of every age believe in the following simple truth: Your life and character are the result of your own thoughts and ideas. In fact, several of the greatest teachers of all time have reinforced the precept that one of the primary secrets of living a life of excellence is simply a matter of thinking thoughts of excellence. In other words, good, strong thoughts will generate good, strong actions. The following qotes reflect that mindset:

"All that a man achieves or fails to achieve is the direct result of his own thoughts"

—Aristotle

"The mind is everything; what you think you become."

—Socrates

"Your life is what your thoughts make it."

—Confucius

"As a man thinketh in his heart, so is he."

—Proverbs 23:7

What is "Character" or "Strength of Will"?

Having "character" or "strength of will" means having the intestinal fortitude to stick to those things that you know to be right and to refuse those things that you know to be wrong. Morals, standards, values, and right and wrong behavior are all intimately related to being a great leader. As a leader of your team and in your everyday life, how should right be distinguished from wrong in both your words and actions?

- Words and actions should help unite, not divide, the members of the team.
- Words and actions should be beneficial and not harmful to team goals.
- Words and actions should help to support, not undermine, the rules and regulations necessary for successful team effort.
- Words and actions should help to strengthen, not weaken, the leadership of the team.
- Words and actions toward the individuals and fans who support the team should always be positive, rather than negative.

Most Importantly, a Leader is Someone Who Can First Lead Himself.

Being a leader begins with "leading yourself." If you want to be a great leader, you must set a great example. If what you say and what you do are two different things, then what you say means nothing. This concept is expressed well by Denis Waitley, in the following poem.

I Would Rather Watch a Winner Than Hear One Any Day

I'd rather watch a winner than hear one any day.
I'd rather have one walk with me than merely show the way.
The eye's a better pupil and more willing than the ear;
Fine counsel is confusing, but example's always clear.
And the best of all the coaches are the ones who live their creeds;
For to see the good in action is what everybody needs.
I can soon learn how to do it if you'll let me see it done;
I can watch your hands in action, but your tongue too fast may run.
And the lectures you deliver may be very wise and true;
But I'd rather get my lessons by observing what you do.
For I may misunderstand you and the high advice you give;
But there's no misunderstanding how you act and how you live.
I'd rather watch a winner than hear one any day!

DO: (15 MINUTES)

* Lead a discussion covering the questions on the worksheet.
* Review the word of the day. Ask a student to use it correctly in a sentence.

Photo Credit: Al Bello/Getty Images Sport

LESSON #2

WHAT IS A LEADER?—WORKSHEET

"Leadership can be described in one word—honesty. You must be honest with the players and honest with yourself. Never be afraid to stick up for your players."
—Earl Weaver

A leader is a person fitted by force of ideas, _____, or by strength of will or administrative ability to arouse, incite, and _____ _____ in conduct and achievement. Most importantly, a leader is someone who can _____.

For discussion:

1. A great leader takes the positive approach. Write down five positive things about your team.

   _____

   _____

   _____

2. What is meant by "character" or "strength of will" in the definition of a leader? Share an example of when you or a fellow team member displayed character.

   _____

   _____

   _____

3. What does the following statement mean to you? "I would rather watch a winner than hear one any day."

   _____

   _____

   _____

Word of the Day: Winner—one who is successful, especially through praiseworthy ability and hard work

200

WHAT IS LEADERSHIP?—COACH'S NOTES

LESSON #3

SAY: (5 MINUTES)

"Leadership is the ability to motivate others, whether by word or deeds, towards desirable behavior."

—Joe Paterno

"The successful leader not only knows where he is going but has the ability to get others to go there with him."

—The Apostle Paul

Leadership is the art of imposing your will upon others in such a manner as to command their respect, confidence, and whole-hearted cooperation. It is the art by which others are caused to carry out the will or decision of the leader. Leadership is the art of getting things accomplished. It requires a person of principles. A team must know what the rules of conduct are, make sure they are right, and then stick to them. No matter how technically proficient a team may be, or how strong or fast, unless the leaders and every member of the team have the knowledge and determination to comply with the rules, the attainment of victory and goals will be extremely difficult. This rule applies off the field, on campus, and in the classroom, cafeteria, and community, as well as to the on-the-field discipline of each individual's assignment on a particular play. Good leadership will help players comply with rules willingly and whole-heartedly. It must be remembered that success does not come easily. Iron-clad determination must be found within the team leaders. Problems will always arise. It is how you handle them as a team that is important.

A successful leader will always take a stand for the best interests of the team. Consider the following example of how leadership can help eliminate problems and keep a team on track. Griping and complaining by a few can make everybody unhappy. Unfortunately, even a very few—one or two players—can create confusion, detract from team goals, and weaken overall effort. These complaints undermine team attitudes and must be resolved among the players through persuasion and education. Suppression will not succeed. Any mistakes by a few must be eliminated by the majority whenever they crop up.

You must truly take a stand for the best interests of the team. If you and the team do not handle these situations properly and relax your guard, the complaints will spread and eventually destroy any chance of team success. The sincere feelings of a team member pertaining to what he considers unjust should be brought to the attention of the coaching staff. If you follow through with this process, team effort will be of such magnitude that success will be inevitable.

DO: (15 MINUTES)

- Lead a discussion on the questions found on the worksheet.
- Review the word of the day. Ask a student to use it correctly in a sentence.

WHAT IS LEADERSHIP?—WORKSHEET

"Knowledge alone is not enough to get desired results. You must have the more elusive ability to teach and to motivate. This defines a leader; if you can't teach and you can't motivate, you can't lead."

—John Wooden

For discussion:

1. What does the following statement mean to you? "No matter how technically proficient a team may be, or how strong or fast, unless the leaders and every member of the team have the knowledge and determination to comply with the rules, the attainment of victory and goals will be extremely difficult." Do you agree? Why or why not?

    _____

    _____

    _____

    _____

2. Identify one outstanding quality of leadership that you see in three of your teammates. Be prepared to share your answers.

    _____

    _____

3. Write down three outstanding qualities of leadership that you see in yourself. In what ways have you already used these qualities to handle tough circumstances?

    _____

    _____

    _____

    _____

    _____

Word of the Day: Respect—a high or special regard; esteem

PRIMARY FACTORS OF A GOOD LEADER— COACH'S NOTES

SAY: (5 MINUTES)

The five primary factors that a person must possess if he is to develop as a leader are covered in this lesson. If you are noticeably lacking in even one aspect, it is highly likely that you will fail as a leader.

❑ *Character*

Character is the first and most important trait of leadership. A person of character is always able to determine right from wrong, and has the courage to adhere to the right. He is a person of honor, a person to be trusted, a person of his word. No man can climb beyond the limitations of his own character.

The Power of Decision

A leader must possess the power of decision, which is the vision to see what must be done, and how and when to do it. This aspect includes several capacities, including:

- A leader must possess judgment so that after considering all factors bearing upon a problem, and the ways to solve it, he can determine the best or most workable solution.
- A leader must possess reasoning skills if good judgment is to be attained.
- A leader must have foresight so that the actions or reactions concerning his decisions may be anticipated.
- A leader must have the capacity to determine the important things and do those things first.
- A leader must have the strength of character to make decisions at the proper time—the time that will create the necessary results.

❑ *The Wisdom to Plan and Order*

Once a decision is reached, the next step is the development of a plan to implement it. This plan should cover the following:

- What is to be done?
- Who will do it?
- Where will it be done?
- When will it be done?
- How will it be done?

❑ *The Courage to Act*

A leader who has the power to make sound decisions and develop plans based upon those decisions may still be far from achieving his goals unless he has the courage to act—to initiate the plan, follow the plan, and see it through to completion. The leader must know the right thing to do and possess the strength of character to do it, despite all the costs, hardships, and hazards.

❏ *The Capacity to Manage*

The capacity to manage simply means making the best use of what you have to accomplish what is required. Effective leaders create the feeling of working "together," rather than "for someone."

DO: (15 MINUTES)

*   Discuss the questions found on the student worksheet.
*   Review the word of the day. Ask a student to use it correctly in a sentence.

Photo Credit: Jamie Squire/Getty Images Sport

PRIMARY FACTORS OF A GOOD LEADER— WORKSHEET

"Leadership, like coaching, is fighting for the hearts and souls of men and getting them to believe in you."

—Eddie Robinson

For discussion:

1. Why is character the first and most important factor a person must possess to be a good leader?

_____

_____

2. What does the following statement mean to you? "No man can climb beyond the limitations of his own character."

_____

_____

3. You possess a potent force that you either use or misuse hundreds of times every day. The greatest power that a person possesses is the power of decision, or the power to choose. What capacities are included in making a powerful decision?

_____

_____

4. Why must a person possess the following traits if he is to develop as a leader?

   • The wisdom to plan and order: _____

   _____

   • The courage to act: _____

   _____

   • The capacity to manage: _____

   _____

Word of the Day: Wisdom—ability to discern inner qualities and relationships; insight

LESSON #5

THE MARKS OF GOOD LEADERSHIP (PART 1)— COACH'S NOTES

SAY: (10 MINUTES)

The manner of executing good leadership varies as much as the people on your team. Good leadership is not about how it's achieved. Good leadership is about what is achieved. It is simply a matter of results. The next several lessons cover 16 characteristics or marks of good leadership.

❏ *A Leader Must Know His Job*

A leader should be skilled in the techniques of his position to the fullest of his physical and mental abilities. Leaders must be able to identify what is required in any situation. Knowing your position allows others to gain confidence in you. In addition, self-confidence makes it easier for others to follow you. Knowledge is fundamental to leadership. No one makes it alone. You gain your knowledge from others. After you have succeeded, look back to see if you might help others do the same. You can never fully pay back those who have helped you, but what you can do is follow their example and help younger players get started. Share your knowledge, experience, and enthusiasm with others. *Leave something behind.* Consider the wisdom expressed in this poem.

The Bridge Builder

*An old man going down a lone highway Came in the evening cold and gray
To a chasm vast and deep and wide
Through which was flowing a sullen tide.*

*The old man crossed in the twilight dim; That swollen stream held no fears for him;
But he turned when safe on the other side
And built a bridge to span the tide.*

*"Old man," said a fellow pilgrim near,
"You are wasting your strength with building here;
Your journey will end with the ending day;
You never again must pass this way;
You have crossed the chasm deep and wide—
Why build you this bridge at the eventide?"*

*The builder lifted his old gray head,
"Good friend, in the path I have come," he said,
"There followed after me today
A youth whose feet must pass this way.
This swollen stream which was naught to me
To that fair-haired youth may a pitfall be;
He, too, must cross in the twilight dim;
Good friend, I am building the bridge for him."*

❑ *A Leader Must Be a Good Teacher*

A leader first determines the job to be done and the best means to do it. Thereafter, he observes, corrects, advises, and stimulates. Teaching, or imparting acquired knowledge to others, may be the highest of human arts, for without it knowledge would be lost and all progress stopped. It is in this phase that upper classmen can help out younger players. They know the job at hand and how to get it done. They must help teach younger players what is expected of them on and off the field; teach them everything they were taught about winning; teach them about class; teach them how to overcome adversity; and teach them the team's style of play. By helping others, you will also help yourself. As these young players grow emotionally, physically, and spiritually, so will you. Nothing can replace the pure self-satisfaction of knowing that your love, time, care, and concern helped someone else grow.

❑ *A Leader Must Display Courage*

Courage means having the strength of character to choose the proper way to do something. It could be more dangerous, more difficult, or more unpleasant—but you will follow the right path instead of the easier paths that entice others to failure. When dealing with your teammates, it takes great courage to say, "What you are doing is incorrect. This is the way to do it right." Such intervention is needed, however, if the team is going to attempt to help each other and maintain consistency throughout the organization.

Courage is the trait that empowers you to be yourself, follow your conscience (instincts), and pursue your vision. Keep in mind that as a leader, courage is not something you pursue; it's something you embody. Courage is not the absence of fear; it's confronting your fears. Vince Lombardi Jr. says, "Courage means experiencing your fear, labeling it for what it is, acknowledging that you're afraid, and, if it's important enough to you, pushing ahead in spite of your fear."

The key point is that you can't be an effective leader without courage. Courage enables you to bring out the best in yourself and to inspire the best in your teammates. Part of that courage is the ability to handle the criticism that comes with achievement. It is a hard precept to understand that even achievement is likely to be criticized. Albert Einstein wrote, "It is an odd occurrence to me that the more my abilities came to light, the more famous I became, the more those abilities were brought into question."

❑ *A Leader Must Display a Capacity to Get Things Done*

The best reputation a player can build is to have it said of him that he "gets the job done." Remember, you cannot build your reputation on things you are *going to do*.

Have the desire, determination, and dedication to get the job done. It is very easy to get sidelined or distracted, so it is important to keep your mind focused on your goals and nothing else. No shortcuts exist in the world of athletics. Athletics is made up of goals to be reached, competitions to be faced, and adversity to overcome. Only the truly dedicated athletes attain their goals. The true test of all great leaders is that they have the capacity to get the job done—they don't let anything interfere with their goals. That is why so few become champions.

DO: (15 MINUTES)

- Lead a discussion of the questions on the worksheet.
- Review the word of the day. Ask a student to use it correctly in a sentence.

Photo Credit: Jonathan Daniel/Getty Images Sport

THE MARKS OF GOOD LEADERSHIP (PART 1)— WORKSHEET

"For a leader, courage involves more than single, isolated acts of bravery or fortitude. Rather, courage is the personal strength that enables leaders to handle fear, make difficult decisions, take risks, confront change, accept responsibility, and be self-reliant."

—Brian Billick

For discussion:

1. Do you believe that knowledge is fundamental to leadership? Why or why not?

   _____

   _____

2. What does the following statement mean? "Teaching, or imparting acquired knowledge to others, may be the highest of human arts, for without it all knowledge would be lost, and all progress stopped."

   _____

   _____

3. Do you agree with the statement in Question #2? Why or why not?

   _____

   _____

4. Give an example of how having the courage to take a stand or avoid obstacles has affected your life.

   _____

   _____

5. What does the following statement mean to you? "You cannot build your reputation on things you are going to do."

   _____

   _____

Word of the Day: Progress—a forward or onward movement, as to an objective or goal

THE MARKS OF GOOD LEADERSHIP (PART 2)— COACH'S NOTES

SAY: (5 MINUTES)

Does anyone remember the marks of leadership that were covered in Lesson #5? (*Note*: A Leader Must Know His Job; A Leader Must Be a Good Teacher; A Leader Must Display Courage; A Leader Must Display a Capacity to Get Things Done). This lesson covers one additional leadership trait.

❏ *A Leader Must Know the People He Is Leading*

It is important to have personal acquaintances with as many members of your team as possible. The more close, personal friendships that grow between members of your squad, the stronger it will be. It is sometimes difficult to convince team members that everyone is of importance to the team. This concept can be easier to teach if friendships exist.

Friendships form a vital and exciting part of life. Everyone has a natural desire to be accepted. An old proverb states, "A man who has friends must himself be friendly." The best way to make a friend is to be a friend. A true friend helps you when you are in trouble. He appreciates you despite your faults, shares in your sorrows, and delights in your success. A true friend will suffer for your sake, defend your name against critics, and always have your best interests at heart. Wouldn't you love to have or be a friend like that? The following tips will help you form strong friendships.

When a new kid comes to your school, show him around. Sacrifice some of your time to help him adjust and go out of your way to make him feel welcome. If a girl is being made fun of or ignored because she is "different" in some way, don't go along with the crowd. Go and help her. If you champion the cause of somebody in need, you will probably win a friend for life.

When a friend wins a prize, is selected for a team, or achieves an honor, celebrate with him. If someone does well on a class assignment or at a sport, for example, make an effort to praise him.

Another key to making friends is to not always be trying to impress. Instead of trying to impress others, just be yourself. Don't be overly opinionated, but don't be overly worried about what others may think of you. Achieving this balance sometimes means daring to be different.

This next tip may seem like a paradox: To become the kind of person that attracts true friends, you must be able and willing to go it alone, if necessary. If your motivation is entirely based on what others think of you, then you will never develop the strength of character needed to attract true friends. True friends are people who respect you for your qualities. If you decide to take an unpopular stand and someone helps and supports you, then you know that you have made a true friend, not the type who will desert you when things get rough.

One more thing: Don't forget to be a true friend to those younger than you. While you may look up to adults as role models, you too may be looked up to as a role model by younger children. If a younger kid needs your help, advice, or friendship, freely give it, but with wisdom. If you don't know how to help, then send your younger friend to the most capable person you can think of.

You can make an impact in the lives of those younger than you. Remember, they need friends as well.

DO: (15 MINUTES)

- Lead a discussion of Questions #1–4 on the worksheet. Give the students time to complete Questions #5, but they do not need to share those answers out loud.
- Review the word of the day. Ask a student to use it correctly in a sentence.

Photo Credit: Jed Jacobsohn/Getty Images Sport

LESSON #6

THE MARKS OF GOOD LEADERSHIP (PART 2)— WORKSHEET

"A cynic is a man who knows the price of everything and the value of nothing."
—Oscar Wilde

For discussion:

1. List five qualities of a true friend.

   _____

   _____

2. How many of the qualities listed in your answer to Question #1 can you honestly say you exhibit on a regular basis?

   _____

   _____

3. Identify a quality that you would like to develop to make yourself a better friend. List three action steps you can take to begin to develop that quality.

   _____

   _____

4. List two true friends you have on the team and one quality you admire about each of them. Be prepared to share your answer.

   _____

   _____

5. List two people on the team with whom you would like to become better friends. What is one step you can take to achieve that? (This answer is confidential.)

   _____

   _____

Word of the Day: Cynic—one who attributes all actions to selfish motives

THE MARKS OF GOOD LEADERSHIP (PART 3)— COACH'S NOTES

LESSON #7

SAY: (5 MINUTES)

The past two lessons have examined the marks of good leadership. Who can tell me one mark? (Note: A Leader Must Know His Job; A Leader Must Be a Good Teacher; A Leader Must Display Courage; A Leader Must Display a Capacity to Get Things Done; A Leader Must Know the People He Is Leading). This lesson examines three more traits of good leadership.

❑ *A Leader Must Set the Standard*

Leaders must set the standards in all things. They must demonstrate self-confidence in being able to get the job done successfully. Doubt in the mind of a leader will always create doubt in the minds of those who look up to him. Can the following be said of you? "He practices to win," or "He plays to win." If everyone on the team works as hard, practices as hard, and plays a hard as you do, how good will the team be? You set the standard.

True leaders are molded from the highest character and are generally the hardest workers on the team. They are the first to come to practice and the last ones to leave. During practice, they lead by example. Leadership is a matter of having people look at you and gaining confidence by seeing how you respond, how you act, and how you live your life.

The principle of setting the standard applies to the little things as well. Courtesy and respect to those you deal with in the training room, equipment room, cafeteria, and classroom set the standard. Promptness for class, meetings, and practices sets the standard for enthusiasm and eagerness to learn and work on the field. In these areas, leaders must step to the front.

❑ *A Leader Must Be Determined*

What is needed on any team are people who say, "All I know for sure is that it's going to get done." Every team needs students who can see the right course, then drive on with determination to its final achievement. A leader is someone who can set his goals, commit himself to those goals, and then pursue them with all of his abilities. This trait requires that you believe in yourself, make self-sacrifices, work hard, and maintain the determination to perform to the best of your ability. Nothing can stop you from being a winner if you really give it all you've got.

Glenn Cunningham's story tells of great determination. After suffering severe burns on his legs at the age of five, Glenn Cunningham was given up by doctors as a hopeless cripple who would spend the rest of his life in a wheelchair. "He will never be able to walk again," they said. "No chance." The doctors examined his legs, but they had no way of looking into Glenn Cunningham's heart. He wouldn't listen to the doctors and set out to walk again. Lying in bed with skinny, red legs covered with scar tissue, Glenn vowed, "Next week, I'm going to get out of bed. I'm going to walk." And he did just that.

His mother tells of how she used to push back the curtain and look out the window to watch Glenn as he would reach up and take hold of an old plow in the yard. With a hand on each handle, he began to make those gnarled and twisted legs function. And despite the pain in every step, he came closer and closer to walking. Soon he began to trot; before long, he was running. When he started to run, he became even more determined. "I always believed that I could walk again, and I did. Now I'm going to run faster than anybody has ever run." And did he ever! He became a great miler who, in 1934, set the world's record of 4:06.8 and was honored as the outstanding athlete of the century at Madison Square Garden. With his desire, Glenn Cunningham wasn't going to spend his life in a wheelchair. No chance!

❑ *A Leader Must Possess Foresight*

To be a great leader, you need the ability to foresee what will likely confront you this afternoon, tomorrow, next week, and next month. By doing so, you will avoid surprises and careless, spur-of-the-moment decisions. Spend time thinking and evaluating your actions before acting. A leader must be able to give up little pleasures in the short-term to achieve the ultimate goal down the road. Make decisions now about temptations that you will face tomorrow and then have the courage to stick to your decision.

One of the greatest lessons in athletics is that you must discipline your life. No matter how good you may be, you must be willing to cut out of your life those things that keep you from getting to the top.

DO: (15 MINUTES)

- Discuss the questions on the worksheet.
- Review the word of the day. Ask a student to use it correctly in a sentence.

THE MARKS OF GOOD LEADERSHIP (PART 3)— WORKSHEET

LESSON #7

"Good coaching is based purely in leadership ... a positive example ... instilling respect in your players."

—John Wooden

For discussion:

1. List at least five examples of standards you can demonstrate to the younger players on this team that will make the team stronger.

_____

_____

_____

_____

_____

2. Who was Glenn Cunningham and what made him special?

_____

_____

_____

_____

3. How can planning, preparing, and possessing foresight strengthen your ability to be a strong leader?

_____

_____

_____

_____

Word of the Day: Foresee—to see a development before it occurs

THE MARKS OF GOOD LEADERSHIP (PART 4)— COACH'S NOTES

LESSON #8

SAY: (5 MINUTES)

The past few lessons have taught you how to recognize good leadership. You now know that a leader must be a good teacher, display courage, display a capacity to get things done, set the standard, and be determined. This lesson covers two more leadership traits.

❑ *A Leader Must Possess Initiative*

Initiative is the "power of commencing." Getting started is the key, because if you want to be successful, you must make the start. The willingness to act is the first step on the path to greatness. It has often been said that, "It's a winner who finds a way to get the job done."

The courage to begin separates dreamers from achievers. The common conception is that motivation leads to action, but the reverse is true—action precedes motivation. You have to take the first step and get the juices flowing, which motivates you to work on your goals. Getting momentum going is the most difficult part of any job, and taking the first step is often what generates greatness.

It Couldn't Be Done

Somebody said that it couldn't be done;
But he with a chuckle replied
That maybe it couldn't, but he would be one
Who wouldn't say so till he'd tried
So he buckled right in with a bit of a grin
On his face. If he worried he hid it.
And he started to sing as he tackled the thing
That couldn't be done—and he did it.

Somebody scoffed, "Oh, you'll never do that.
At least no one ever has done it."
But he took off his coat and he took off his hat.
And the first thing we knew he'd begun it.
Well, he buckled right in with a bit of a grin,
Without any doubting or quiddit,
And he started to sing as he tackled the thing
That couldn't be done—and he did it.

There are thousands to tell you it can't be done,
There are thousands to prophesy failure
And thousands to point out to you, one by one
The dangers that wait to assail you.

But just buckle in—with a bit of a grin;
Just take off your coat and go to it.
And start to sing as you tackle the thing
That "cannot be done" and you'll do it.

—Edgar Guest

❑ *A Leader Must Excel in Teamwork*

Teamwork is action coordinated with others. Realize that your talents must be blended with the talents of your teammates for the unit to function effectively. Every player on a team is an extension of the other players. So if one player shines in a given game, he is an extension of all the guys who helped him prepare for the game—even those who may not be able to play themselves. You are all an extension of each other.

Many people have commented on this concept. For example, Vince Lombardi once said, "Individual commitment to a group effort—that is what makes a team work, a company work, a society work, a civilization work." Lombardi also said, "Teamwork is what the Green Bay Packers were all about. They did not do it for individual glory. They did it because they loved one another."

Jack Whitaker observed, "The sports world is a classic example of the game of life. Much can be accomplished when nobody becomes too concerned with who gets the credit. Great players are made possible by unselfish and disciplined individuals who are more concerned with end results than with personal ones."

John Wooden is quoted as saying, "The main ingredient of stardom is the rest of the team." Remember, the finest compliment that anyone can pay a player is to say, "He is a complete team player." To deserve this tribute, your every thought, action, and deed should be done for the team.

Law of the Jungle

Now this is the Law of the Jungle—
As old and as true as the sky;
And the wolf that keeps it may prosper,
But the wolf that shall break it must die.
And the vine that girdles the tree trunk,
The law runneth forward and back—
And the strength of the pack is the wolf
And the strength of the wolf is the pack.

—Rudyard Kipling

DO: (15 MINUTES)

- Discuss the questions on the worksheet.
- Review the word of the day. Ask a student to use it correctly in a sentence.

THE MARKS OF GOOD LEADERSHIP (PART 4)— WORKSHEET

"It is better to deserve honors and not have them than to have them and not deserve them."

—Mark Twain

For discussion:

1. What is initiative?

    _____

    _____

    _____

    _____

2. What message do you believe Ralph Waldo Emerson was offering when he said, "We are always getting ready to live, but never living."

    _____

    _____

    _____

    _____

3. What does the following statement mean? "Great players are made possible by unselfish and disciplined individuals who are more concerned with end results than with personal ones." Do you agree? Why or why not?

    _____

    _____

    _____

    _____

Word of the Day: Honor—recognition or distinction

THE MARKS OF GOOD LEADERSHIP (PART 5)— COACH'S NOTES

LESSON #9

SAY: (5 MINUTES)

This lesson continues to break down what constitutes good leadership by detailing two additional qualities of a great leader.

❑ *A Leader Must Be Consistent*

Instant success is never possible. Greatness results only from sustained, consistent, self-disciplined effort over an extended period of time. Consistency is what counts; you have to be able to do things right over and over again. Plenty of people can do good work for a short while with immediate gratification in mind, but for a leader, good work must become a habit.

Consistency is the truest measure of performance. Almost anyone can have a great day or a good year, but true success is the ability to perform day in and day out, year after year, under all kinds of conditions. Inconsistency may win some of the time. Consistency will win most of the time.

Consistency requires concentration, determination, and repetition. To be at your best all of the time, you must do the following:

- Take nothing for granted. If you are not "up" every day, something or someone will knock you down.
- Take pride in what you know. The things you do well are the things you enjoy doing.
- Take setbacks in stride. Don't brood over reverses; learn from them.
- Take calculated chances. To win something, you must risk something.
- Take work home. To get ahead, plan ahead.
- Take the extra lap. Condition yourself for the long run. The tested can always take it.
- Don't take "no" for an answer. You can do what you believe you can.

❑ *A Leader Must Be Calm in a Crisis*

A player who shows a lack of confidence in a critical situation will communicate that feeling to his teammates. Do not depart from the thing that counts—do your very best at all times and believe that you will get the job done.

The secret to having poise and confidence is preparation. By practicing, you come to a point of competence. You will find yourself accomplishing your goal gracefully and confidently. It is then that you do things that you never dreamed you could do. You discover powers you never knew existed. Great leaders maintain their poise and concentration when they are staring defeat in the face.

When the Pressure's On

How do you act when the pressure's on?
When the chance for victory is almost gone,
When Fortune's star has refused to shine,
When the ball is on your 5-yard line?
How do you act when the going's rough?
Does your spirit lag when breaks are tough?
Or is there in you a flame that flows
Brighter as fiercer the battle grows?
How hard, how long will you fight the foe?
That's what the world would like to know
Cowards can fight when they're out ahead...
The uphill grind knows a thoroughbred!
Do you wish for success? Then tell me, son—
How do you act when the pressure's on?

—J. Fred Lawton

DO: (15 MINUTES)

* Discuss the questions found on the worksheet.
* Review the word of the day. Ask a student to use it correctly in a sentence.

Photo Credit: Al Bello/Getty Images Sport

THE MARKS OF GOOD LEADERSHIP (PART 5)— WORKSHEET

"The ability to keep a cool head in an emergency, maintain poise in the midst of excitement, and to refuse to be stampeded are the true marks of leadership."

—R. Shannon

For discussion:

1. Why is it important to be consistent?

   _____

   _____

   _____

   _____

2. To be at your best, one of the things suggested was to take setbacks in stride. Recall one setback you've had and what you learned from it. Be prepared to share your answer.

   _____

   _____

   _____

   _____

3. How does preparation generate poise?

   _____

   _____

   _____

   _____

Word of the Day: Poise—A stable, balanced state; gracious tact in coping or handling a situation

THE MARKS OF GOOD LEADERSHIP (PART 6)— COACH'S NOTES

SAY: (5 MINUTES)

This lesson presents two additional characteristics of good leadership.

❑ *A Leader Must Be Adept at Overcoming Difficulties*

Somehow, true leaders rise out of the mud. When you are faced with a problem or difficulty, you have two options: You can quit and walk away or you can stay and meet the challenge head-on. In reality, adversity is a reality of life. You are never really sure when it will come or how long it will stay, but the way each person handles tough situations in his life is a direct reflection of the character he possesses. The real test of a person does not come when everything is going well. The real test comes after adversity has struck.

Adversity can be a great motivator. In athletics, as in anything else, a series of difficulties always occurs. Your success will depend on how well you are prepared and how well you handle those problems as they come along. Coach John Wooden said, "Things turn out best for those who make the best of the way things turn out." The key is to concentrate your way through the bad times. You can have some of your best games that way. You perform better because you have to concentrate harder when you are facing adversity.

It may sound strange, but champions are made champions by setbacks. They are champions because they have been hurt. Their experience moved them and pulled out a fighting spirit, making them what they are. Sometimes in life you are given a challenge to bring out your fighting spirit. Everything that happens to you can happen for good if you have this spirit. The essential thing is not in the conquering, but in the fight.

❑ *A Leader Must Require Discipline*

First, you must require discipline of yourself, and then your teammates. Athletes who are part of a disciplined group will each do their full share, so that the team will achieve its goals and objectives. A player can best require discipline of his teammates through inspiration—by making clear the reasons team goals are important.

Whether the game is scoreless or tied, or you are ahead or behind by a few points, it takes a disciplined team to play in a tight situation. You need team members who will each continue to do their part, knowing that the only way your ultimate goal can be reached is through disciplined effort. Remember, "He that has learned to obey will know how to command."

One of the greatest lessons you can learn in athletics is that you must discipline your life. No matter how good you may be, you must cut out those things that keep you from getting to the top. The people who accomplish great things in life are willing to discipline their lives and maintain their health, vitality, and efficiency through a process of rigorous discipline.

Bobby Knight said it this way: "It has always been my thought that the most important single ingredient to success in athletics or life is discipline. I have many times felt that this word is the most ill-defined in all of our language. My definition of the word is as follows: Do what has to be done; when it has to be done; as well as it can be done; and do it that way all the time."

DO: (15 MINUTES)

* Discuss the questions on the worksheet.
* Review the word of the day. Ask a student to use it correctly in a sentence.

Photo Credit: Ronald Martinez/Getty Images Sport

THE MARKS OF GOOD LEADERSHIP (PART 6)— WORKSHEET

"A wise man will make more opportunities than he finds."

—Francis Bacon

For discussion:

1. What difficulty has your team recently faced? How have you overcome it? How has it made you a better team?

   _____

   _____

   _____

2. What does the following statement mean to you? "Things work out best for those who make the best of the way things work out."

   _____

   _____

   _____

3. Why is discipline an important factor in leadership?

   _____

   _____

   _____

4. Identify one area in which you need more discipline (e.g., schoolwork, study habits, physical conditioning, language, food choices). What is one thing you can do today to begin practicing discipline in that area?

   _____

   _____

   _____

Word of the Day: Inspiration—the action or power of moving the intellect or emotions

THE MARKS OF GOOD LEADERSHIP (PART 7)— COACH'S NOTES

LESSON #11

SAY: (5 MINUTES)

The past several lessons have examined the qualities that collectively help constitute good leadership. This lesson concludes the topic by reviewing the last two leadership traits.

❑ *A Leader Must Accept Full Responsibility*

A leader is responsible for all that his team does—or fails to do. Do not be afraid to say, "It was my fault," and praise your teammates in time of success. The day an athlete takes complete responsibility for himself and stops making any excuses is the day he starts his climb to the top. On every play, you are the one who has to wear the hat. You have to make it happen. You have to take responsibility for yourself, and you have to take responsibility for your team.

The word "if" should be eliminated from a leader's vocabulary. So many young athletes lament their lack of success by saying, "If I were bigger; if I were faster; if I had more strength; if I had a better coach; if I had more experience." The success that the great ones achieve comes because they accepted responsibility, dedicated themselves to excellence, and utilized whatever physical characteristics they were endowed with. For true leaders, no other course exists except to take responsibility for their own destiny.

If you make a mistake, admit it quickly and emphatically and do not dwell on it. You have to be critical of yourself—though not supercritical—and you have to call the play as it is. Then, you can grow from that experience. If you make excuses for yourself, you are telling yourself that everything is all right. You are going nowhere. You can never let yourself be satisfied. In that regard, Coach Paul "Bear" Bryant once said, "When you make a mistake, there are only three things you should ever do about it: admit it, learn from it, and don't repeat it."

It is your game to win or lose. You alone are responsible. So accept responsibility for your actions as true champions do—and don't make excuses.

❑ *A Leader Must Be Able to Get Along With People*

A leader has the ability to get along with athletes of all ages. He is accepted in group gatherings off the field as well as on the field.

While it is true that you must depend first upon yourself, you need to be able to work with your teammates as well. Pride in yourself has its place as you work with others. Pride influences your actions. Pride—that is, feeling good about your progress, the value of your work, and the excellence of your conduct—helps you go further and do more than you thought possible. After individual pride is developed, group pride, or *esprit de corps*, will follow.

You will gain what you want with the help and support of others. To be agreeable, to be liked, and to cooperate contributes immeasurably to your success. When you coordinate your efforts with the efforts of others, you speed the way to your goals.

Always try to do something for your teammates and you will be surprised by how many things come your way—how many pleasant things are done for you. Henry Ford said it this way: "Coming together is a beginning; keeping together is progress; working together is success." Zig Ziglar expressed the same thing a bit differently: "You can have everything in life you want if you will just help enough other people get what they want."

For you to get along well with others, mutual respect must be present. Respect is an extension of a positive, optimistic attitude. Respect for others begins with respect for self. Respect for team members breeds togetherness. It has no ethnic, racial, or social barriers. Players with respect for one another win together. Respect is also a two-way street between players and coaches. Signs of disrespect have negative influences on a team and can affect your ability to play and win as a team.

Successful teams are a family of one. And on a successful team, no one embarrasses anybody in front of his peers or in public. One formula for building respect is developed through an attitude of:
- PLP = players love players
- CLP = coaches love players
- PLC = players love coaches
- CLC = coaches love coaches

DO: (15 MINUTES)

- Lead a discussion covering the questions on the worksheet.
- Review the word of the day. Ask a student to use it correctly in a sentence.

"THE MARKS OF GOOD LEADERSHIP (PART 7)— WORKSHEET

"If one advances confidently in the direction of his dreams, and endeavors to live the life which he has imagined, he will meet a success unexpected in common hours."

—Henry David Thoreau

For discussion:

1. What are the three things Coach "Bear" Bryant said you should do when you make a mistake?

    _____

    _____

    _____

2. Why is it so important for a leader to take responsibility for himself and his team?

    _____

    _____

    _____

    _____

3. "You can have everything in life you want if you will just help enough other people get what they want." What does this statement mean to you?

    _____

    _____

    _____

    _____

Word of the Day: Endeavor—a concerted effort

YOU AS A LEADER—COACH'S NOTES

LESSON #12

SAY: (5 MINUTES)

Pride influences everything you do. You can be proud of several things, including the following:

- The fact that you are developing into a leader of this team
- The things for which this program stands
- The team (the people that make it up) of which you are part
- The history and tradition of the team
- The traditions of the school
- Being here with purpose—of getting a diploma and playing for this team
- Your country and the ideas for which it stands
- The work that each of you is doing, which is extremely valuable to the team and necessary for the success of the team

Great leaders never, never quit! Why? In a word, pride. They believe in themselves very strongly and feel that they are the best in their sport—bar none. Such feelings drive champions to perfection. They want to be number one—pure and simple. It is their pride that makes them number one and keeps them there.

Pride is developed in an athlete, but you won't gain it with a half-hearted performance. You have to give 100 percent all of the time. When you do, your pride will increase dramatically. Why? Because the more intense your effort, the more intense your pride. The more intense your pride, the more you will want to win.

Stress the positive aspects of your life and eliminate the negative elements. If you do not like what you are doing, do not do it anymore. If you do not feel that you are working hard enough to be proud of yourself, work harder. It is not that difficult. If you really do not like what you see in the mirror, change it. How? By taking responsibility for your own life. If you want to be successful, think, act, and look successful. Taking risks and going beyond the ordinary is the only way to become a winner and have pride in yourself.

When two athletes are equal in terms of natural ability, preparation, conditioning, and reaction to pressure, who will have the edge? Who will win? The answer is simple. The athlete who is at his best, who loves a hard battle, and who refuses to lose will always come out on top. In other words, the athlete with the most pride will win.

No matter what happens—never let an opponent take away your pride. Be proud of your school and your team. Players must be proud of the team to a degree where they will stand up and protect it and its reputation. Players must be proud of their individual positions, their group, and the entire program.

The following story exemplifies the need for pride. Every man in the Old West knew the importance of a brand, which was the mark that a rancher would burn on his stock. But a brand was more than that. When a man hooked up with a certain outfit, it was said that he was "ridin' for the brand."

The term "ridin' for the brand" was an expression of loyalty to the outfit he rode for. If a man did not like the outfit or the way they conducted their affairs, he was free to go, and many did. But if he stayed on, he gave loyalty and he received loyalty. Much was forgiven if a man had loyalty, courage, and integrity, and if he did his job. If a man gave less than his best, somebody else always had to take up the slack.

Your team must reward that kind of loyalty—someone who is "ridin' for the brand." When a player begins to understand the privilege and responsibility of owning his brand, he will give nothing less than his best.

DO: (15 MINUTES)

- Lead a discussion covering the questions on the worksheet.
- Review the word of the day. Ask a student to use it correctly in a sentence.

YOU AS A LEADER—WORKSHEET

"Be the kind of person that you want people to think you are."

—Socrates

For discussion:

1. How can an athlete develop pride in himself?

_____

_____

_____

_____

_____

2. What makes pride such an important part of the competitive spirit of an athlete?

_____

_____

_____

_____

_____

3. What does the term "ridin' for the brand" mean to you?

_____

_____

_____

_____

_____

Word of the Day: Reputation—the general estimation in which a person (or team) is held by the public

DEVELOPING *ESPRIT DE CORPS*—COACH'S NOTES

SAY: (5 MINUTES)

Esprit de corps is the common spirit pervading the members of a body or association of persons. It implies sympathy, enthusiasm, devotion, and disregard of the individual for the sake of the group.

One of the most important traits a leader can possess is unselfishness, to have a team-first mindset. The first task of leadership is to promote and enforce collective loyalty, also known as *esprit de corps*.

American educator Charles Eliot once remarked, "If I had the opportunity to say a final word to all the young people of America, it would be this: Don't think too much about yourself. Try to cultivate the habit of thinking of others; this will reward you. Selfishness always brings its own revenge. It cannot be escaped. Be unselfish. That is the first and final commandment for those who would be useful and happy in their usefulness."

The leaders on your team will work together to create a feeling of unity. This unity will help raise morale, or the collective state of mind of our team. What you as a group think, feel, and believe constitutes morale, whether good or bad.

Morale, then, is confidence that is obtained when players are certain in their own minds that they know their jobs well and that they will win the game. "Confidence does not come out of nowhere. It is a result of something . . . Hours and days and weeks and years of constant work and dedication," said Roger Staubach.

Joe Namath once stated, "What I do is prepare myself until I know I can do what I have to do." On this same topic, Vince Lombardi said, "Confidence comes from planning and practicing well. You get ready during the week and the confidence will be there on game day. This confidence is a difficult thing to explain. But you do get it and the team gets it if you have prepared properly."

Morale breeds confidence. And courage is born of confidence. A man is courageous when he knows what to do and what is expected of him. No great courage can exist where no confidence or assurance is present, and half the battle is in the conviction that you can do what you undertake.

It is easy to be ordinary or mediocre, but it takes courage to excel, to be different from the crowd, which is why not many people can do it. The rewards are great, but so are the risks. It takes courage to sacrifice, to work long, hard hours when you could be relaxing, to work out when you are tired or sick, to focus on being the best when so many distractions are all around you, to seek out tough competition when you know you might get beaten. It is easy to be average, but it is hard to be the best.

It takes courage to stand by your convictions when people around you have no convictions. It takes courage to keep fighting when you are losing. And it takes courage to push yourself to places that you have never been before physically and mentally, to test your limits, to break through barriers.

You were put on this earth to be tested, to be challenged with adversity and see what you can accomplish. A successful person continually faces the problems and challenges that life brings—and overcomes them all, no matter what the obstacle.

Most everyone has far more courage than they give themselves credit for. When tested, people find that they have the courage to look deep into their souls and do things they never thought possible. This ability amazes most people, who initially do not believe they have much courage. You all have it. You just do not realize it.

Finally, a team must have enthusiasm. Enthusiasm comes from appreciation of the worthiness of the cause—the reward that will follow outstanding achievement—accompanied by the determination to get on with the task and receive the prize. Enthusiasm comes from a vision of accomplishment.

Vision is the gift of seeing clearly what may be. Vision expands your horizons. The more you see, the more you can achieve; the grander your vision, the more glorious your accomplishment. The courage to follow your dreams is the first step toward destiny.

DO: (15 MINUTES)

- Lead a discussion covering the questions on the worksheet.
- Review the word of the day. Ask a student to use it correctly in a sentence.

Photo Credit: Brian Bahr/Getty Images Sport

DEVELOPING *ESPRIT DE CORPS*—WORKSHEET

"There is real magic in enthusiasm. It spells the difference between mediocrity and accomplishment."

—Norman Vincent Peale

For discussion:

1. In your own words, what is *esprit de corps*?

_____

_____

_____

_____

2. Why is *esprit de corps* important to leadership?

_____

_____

_____

3. What can you do to increase your confidence level?

_____

_____

_____

4. What can you do to increase enthusiasm in yourself and on the team?

_____

_____

_____

Word of the Day: Unity—the state or quality of being one; singleness

GOALS

Photo Credit: Harry How/Getty Images Sport

Chapter 7

"We find no real satisfaction or happiness in life without obstacles to conquer and goals to achieve.

—Maxwell Maltz

COUNTING THE SQUARES—COACH'S NOTES

SAY: (5 MINUTES)

Zig Ziglar tells a story of flying over Niagara Falls and looking down from six miles in the sky to see and almost "feel" the power of the water cascading to the bottom of the falls. For countless years, this water simply fell to the bottom, beautiful and awesome to the eye—yet totally unproductive. It took a man with a vision and a plan to harness the power of that great waterfall to produce electricity. The power had always been there, but until it was given direction and harnessed, it was worthless.

Many young people enter a sports program in exactly that state. Some have enormous ability and some have limited ability. The quality of a coach is determined by how he takes the ability the athletes have within and "harnesses" it (i.e., give it direction to "light up" the opponents).

No athlete wants to be bad or even mediocre. Every player will say that he wants to be great, but most do not know how to become great. This statement does not apply to highly skilled, self-motivated, disciplined athletes who will succeed no matter who the coach is. It speaks to the athletes who lack "something"—most often a goals program, a plan, a purpose. A coach's job is to give athletes that program, that plan, that purpose. Many label this responsibility as "motivation." The following example from Zig Ziglar's book, See You At the Top, *illustrates this type of motivation.*

(*Note*: This illustration should be drawn on a flip chart, blackboard, or overhead transparency.)

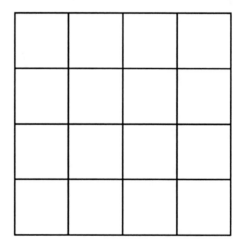

How many squares do you see? (Pause for answers.) If you said 16, you have lots of company. If you said 17, you are in a much more select group, but you are still in error. Count the squares again. (*Note*: See the next page for how to get a total of 30 squares.)

As you can see, 30 squares are found in that diagram. No one added any more squares. It is simply that you now know where they are. That example shows what goal-setting can do for you—point out what is already there.

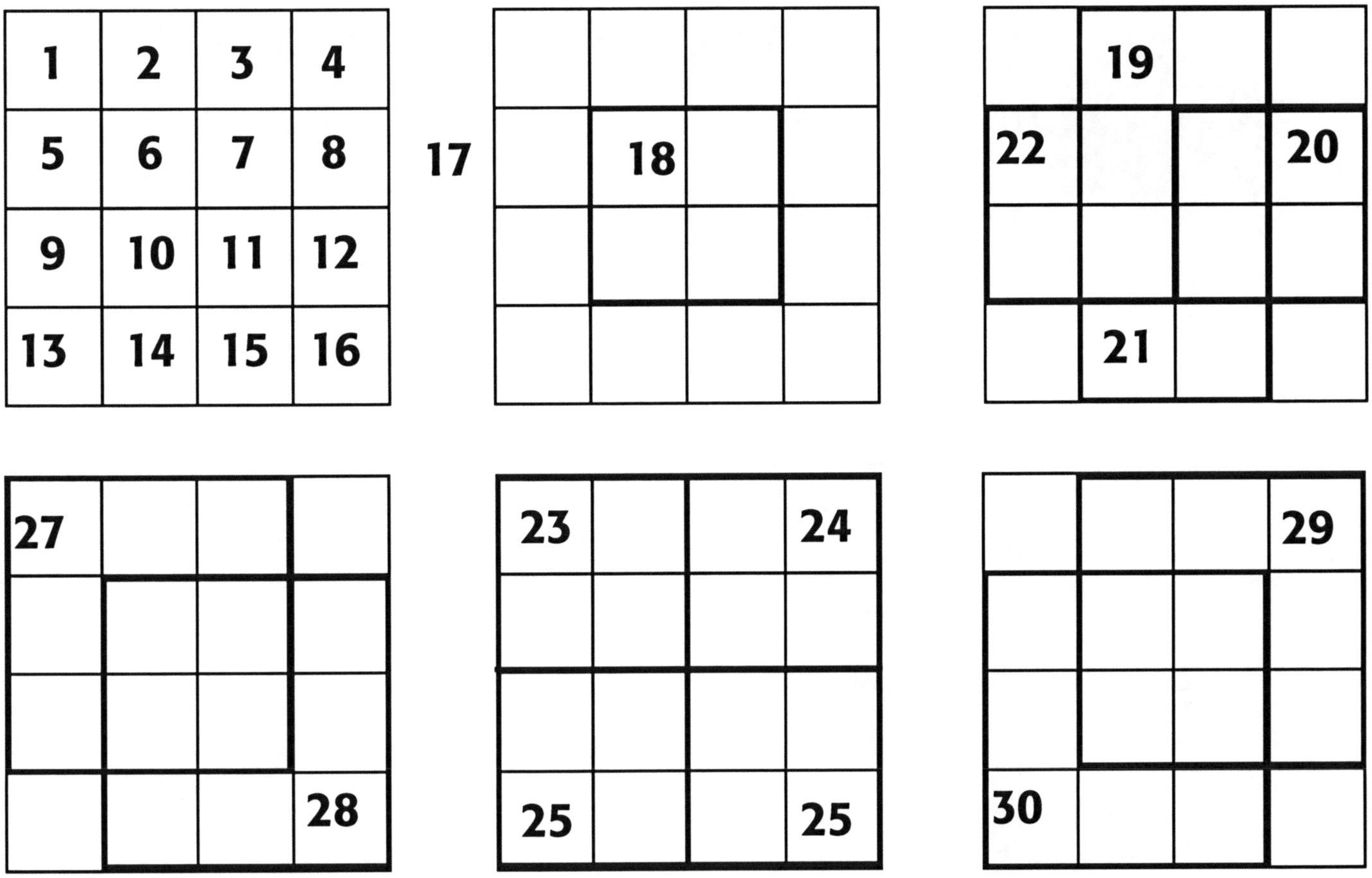

1 2 3 4
5 6 7 8
9 10 11 12
13 14 15 16

17 **18**

19
22 **20**
21

27 **28**

23 **24**
25 **25**

29
30

Many of you have no idea how good you can be—you only know that you want to be good. This goals module will show you how to be your very best. It will give you a direction, a plan, a purpose. None of you can deny that you want to be good. These lessons will help you create that plan. This goals program will not only make you successful in athletics, but by learning the formula and disciplining yourself to the program, you will also be able to transfer that knowledge to your life and use it in whatever you choose to do.

COACHES NOTE

Every coach should pick one player on the team without naming this person to the other coaches and make that athlete his project during this module. Every team has one player who, if he were to reach his potential, would make the team much better. Each coach should write that name on a piece of paper, put it in an envelope, and seal it. Open the envelope at the end of next season.

DO: (15 MINUTES)

- Lead a discussion of the questions found on the student worksheet.
- Review the word of the day. Ask a student to use it correctly in a sentence.

LESSON #1

COUNTING THE SQUARES—WORKSHEET

"Vision is the art of seeing things invisible."

—Jonathan Swift

For discussion:

1. What is the similarity between you and the squares?

_____

_____

_____

_____

2. What does it take to get everything out of you—to get all 30 squares of your ability?

_____

_____

_____

_____

_____

3. Why would someone live his life with only 16 squares?

_____

_____

_____

_____

Word of the Day: Power—the ability to act or produce an effect

IMPORTANCE OF GOALS—COACH'S NOTES

SAY: (5 MINUTES)

How important are goals in your life? It could mean a substantial difference in how much money you make. David Jansen of UCLA conducted a study of people from all walks of life. He found that people who had a goals program made $7,411 monthly, compared to $3,397 monthly for people who had no goals program—a more than $4,000 a month difference. He also found that people with a program were happier, healthier, and had greater peace of mind.

The name Howard Hill probably does not sound familiar to you. He was possibly the greatest archer who ever drew a bow string. He was so accurate that he killed a bull elephant, a Bengal tiger, and a Cape buffalo with a bow and arrow. In newsreels, Howard Hill would repeatedly hit the target dead center. After sending the first arrow to the center of the bull's eye, he would then literally split that arrow with his next shot.

However, any of you could outshoot Howard Hill on the best day he ever had. You could hit the bull's-eye with more consistency than Howard Hill! Obviously, it would be necessary to blindfold him and turn him around a time or two. Then I guarantee that you would have hit the bull's-eye more consistently than he would. I hope that you think the analogy is ridiculous and that you are saying, "Of course, I could! How could a man hit a target that he couldn't see?" That's a good question, but consider this one: If Howard Hill couldn't hit a target he couldn't see, how can you hit a target you don't *have*?

The importance of goals can be understood by looking at a scene from the deciding game of a basketball championship. The teams have taken their warm-up shots and are physically ready for the game. The adrenaline is flowing and it's obvious that the players feel the excitement that goes with a championship game. They return to their dressing rooms and the coach gives them the last "shot in the arm" before action begins. He may say, "This is it, fellows. It's now or never. We win or lose it all tonight. Nobody remembers the best man at the wedding, and nobody remembers who came in second. The whole season is tonight."

The players respond. They're so charged up that they almost tear the doors off the hinges as they rush back to the court. As they get to the court, they stop short in complete confusion, which gives way to frustration and anger as they point out that the goals have been removed. They angrily demand to know how they can play a game without the goals. They know that without goals, they would never know the score, whether they hit or miss, how they stack up against competition, and whether they are on- or off-target. As a matter of fact, they wouldn't even attempt to play the basketball game without the goals. Those basketball goals are important, aren't they? What about you? Are you attempting to play the game of life without goals? If you are, what's the score?

An interesting phenomenon takes place in homes for the elderly. The death rate declines dramatically before holidays and special days, such as wedding anniversaries and birthdays. Many of the residents in these homes set a personal goal to live for one more Christmas, one more anniversary, one more Fourth of July. Immediately after the event—when the goal has been reached—the will to live declines and the death rate shoots upward.

Goals are tools that enable individuals to set the path that they want to follow in life. In other words, they serve as guideposts by which particular courses of action can be advanced and the results of those actions gauged and evaluated. As Maxwell Maltz so aptly put it, "Man is like a bicycle; unless he is moving onward and upward toward a goal, he's going to falter and fall."

DO: (15 MINUTES)

- Lead a discussion covering Questions #1–3 on the worksheet.
- After everyone has written a goal for Question #4, ask for some volunteers to share what they will be working on this week.
- Review the word of the day. Ask a student to use it correctly in a sentence.

IMPORTANCE OF GOALS—WORKSHEET

"There are those who travel and those who are going somewhere. They are different, and yet they are the same. The successful man has this over his rivals: He knows where he is going."

—Mark Caine

For discussion:

1. Why are goals important?

_____

_____

_____

2. Why do you think most people don't set goals?

_____

_____

_____

3. For every reason you listed for Question #2, develop a plan to overcome that excuse.

_____

_____

_____

4. Write down one goal that, with some effort, you can accomplish this week.

_____

_____

_____

Word of the Day: Value—worth, utility, or importance

WHY PEOPLE DON'T SET GOALS—COACH'S NOTES

SAY: (5 MINUTES)

Do most people have goals? Apparently not. You can stop a hundred young people on any street and ask each one, "What are you doing that will absolutely guarantee your failure in life?" After recovering from their initial shock, each one will probably say, "What do you mean, 'what am I doing to guarantee my failure?' I'm working for success." Tragically, most of them think they are. Almost everyone believes they will make it, but the odds are against them. This point must be emphasized, because if you followed those one hundred young people until they were 65 years old, only five of them will have achieved financial security. Only one will be wealthy. The odds are against them.

Failure is not caused by lack of opportunity, because life offers many unique opportunities. For example, several years ago, a wealthy person was released from the federal prison in Atlanta, Georgia. He had a built-in "loser's limp." Nevertheless, he had accumulated a small fortune by operating a tailor shop in prison. After his big mistake had landed him in prison, he was determined not to make a bigger one by "serving time." He made time "serve" him. In a real sense, you have the same choice.

Do the people in life who don't succeed actually plan to fail? No. The problem is that they don't plan anything. If goals are so important, why do only 3 percent of Americans specifically commit their goals to paper? The remaining 97 percent are like ships without rudders. Each will drift and not drive. These 97 percent end up on the beaches of despair—defeated and despondent.

What most of these rudderless people fail to realize is that success is not a spectator sport. Action is the foundation of accomplishment. No one can expect to arrive at success without having made the trip. Certainly, Sir Edmund Hillary, the first man to climb Mount Everest, if asked how he did it, would not have replied, "I was just wandering around one day and ended up on top."

Three reasons are cited for why people don't set goals. The first reason is that they have never been sold on the importance of goals. Everyone is told; only 3 percent are sold. Everyone will tell you that they believe goals are important, but only 3 percent believe it enough to write them down. You need to change "believing" to "be living." You have to do before you can have. If you are not sold, when will you be?

The second reason is that they don't know how to execute a goals program. You will not have this excuse when you complete these lessons. And third, they fear they won't reach the goals they set and will be embarrassed.

If fear is your problem, it simply means that you don't want to be wrong in front of your friends, so you won't make a commitment. By the way, you are half right in this approach: Never share your "go-up" goals with anyone unless you know they not only believe you can reach those goals, but also *want* you to reach them. Share your "give-up" goals (tobacco, cursing) with everyone.

Others decide not to commit their goals to paper so that if they don't quite "make it," they will have a built-in explanation that they didn't really fail because they never set firm goals. This practice is a safe, and even "no-risk," approach for them.

Using that line of reasoning, it would be "safe" for a ship to stay in the harbor, because a ship encounters "risk" when it heads out to sea. But the ship will collect barnacles and become unseaworthy even more quickly by staying in the harbor.

Yes, danger is inherent in setting goals, but the risk is infinitely greater when you don't set goals. The reason is simple. Just as ships are built to sail, so is a person created for a purpose. That purpose is to get everything out of yourself that is humanly possible so that you can make your contribution to mankind. Goals enable you to do for yourself and others.

DO: (15 MINUTES)

- Lead a discussion of Questions #1 and #2 found on the worksheet.
- Allow time for each student to complete Question #3, but do not ask for answers.
- Review the word of the day. Ask a student to use it correctly in a sentence.

Photo Credit: Jonathan Daniel/Getty Images Sport

LESSON #3

WHY PEOPLE DON'T SET GOALS—WORKSHEET

"A soul without a high goal is like a ship without a rudder."

—Eileen Caddy

For discussion:

1. What does the following statement mean to you? "Action is the foundation of accomplishment."

    _____

    _____

    _____

    _____

2. How do you plan to never become like a ship stuck in the harbor?

    _____

    _____

    _____

    _____

3. Confidentially, what is holding you back from setting goals in every area of your life? What could help you overcome those reasons?

    _____

    _____

    _____

    _____

Word of the Day: Plan—a method for achieving an end

GOAL COMMITMENT—COACH'S NOTES

SAY: (10 MINUTES)

Because most people understand how important goals are, the fact that only three percent put them down in writing makes you realize that more goes into goal setting than simply "setting a goal." If you understand the importance and learn how to set goals, you will be one of the three percent. So what exactly is a goal?

A vision with no action is a "dream." Everyone knows a person living this way. He is always talking about what he is going to do, yet you never seeing him taking any steps or doing anything to get what he says he wants. These people are dreamers and are not taken seriously by themselves or their friends—and are loved by their opponents.

Work without a vision is "drudgery." Athletes who live this way have no vision, no goal, no dream. They work out today because they did so yesterday. They do what they have to do. They are not working to get somewhere. They are working to satisfy the coach.

Vision with work is a "goal." A person who lives this way has a destination, but understands that if you don't propel yourself toward that destination you will never get there. Will Rogers said, "You might be on the right track, but if you just sit there, you will get run over."

Consider this story of two men, one with a goal and one without. Several years ago, on an extremely hot day, a railroad crew was working on the roadbed of the railroad when they were interrupted by a slow-moving train. The train ground to a stop and a window in the last car, which incidentally was custom-made and air-conditioned, was raised. A booming, friendly voice called out, "Dave, is that you?" Dave Anderson, the crew chief, called back, "Sure is, Jim, and it's really good to see you."

With that pleasant exchange, Dave Anderson was invited to join Jim Murphy, the president of the railroad, for a visit. For more than an hour, the men exchanged pleasantries and then shook hands as the train pulled out. Dave Anderson's crew immediately surrounded him and everyone expressed astonishment that he knew Jim Murphy, the president of the railroad, as a personal friend. Dave then explained that more than 20 years earlier, he and Jim Murphy had started to work for the railroad on the same day. One of the men, half-jokingly and half-seriously, asked Dave why he was still working out in the hot sun and Jim Murphy had gotten to be president. Rather wistfully, Dave explained, "Twenty-three years ago, I went to work for $1.75 an hour and Jim Murphy went to work for the railroad."

You have left many Dave Andersons behind. Think back to earlier grades. How many of your friends were participating in athletics? Many of them were there for $1.75 an hour, meaning that they participated because of their parents, their brothers, or because they thought they would see what it was like. You are the Jim Murphys of athletics, but the longer you stay in athletics, the more you have to give to keep getting. You are at a point right now where you are going to have to make the commitment to get to the next level. Just being here is not enough. You have to develop a vision. You have to work for the railroad—the team—to get everything you want. If you will make the commitment, you can be the president, meaning that you can get to the next level.

Until this point, you could simply be a "wandering generality" and just do as the program dictated. Now you must develop a vision. You have to make the commitment to:
- Learn how to set goals
- Discipline yourself daily to follow a plan to reach the goal

The following story reinforces the value of setting goals and adhering to them. Two boys made a bet about who could walk the farthest on the railroad tracks. One boy was very heavy and one was of average weight. The heavy boy could seemingly walk forever, while the more athletic boy could go only a few steps before he would fall off. The athlete constantly looked down at his feet and would fall. The other boy would fix his eyes on a point down the track and start walking toward that point. As he came closer to that point, he would find another point farther down the track and start walking toward that new point.

The commitment that you need to make is simple: Don't look at the obstacles or what might go wrong. Set a point on the "railroad track" of this year and start moving toward it. When the whole team gets to that point, reestablish a new point and keep going forward. You simply need to make the commitment to set the "vision" and start walking.

DO: (10 MINUTES)

- Have each team member fill out the worksheet (they should not choose their partner yet).
- Read aloud the three paragraphs at the bottom of the worksheet.
- Have each student pick a partner. (Make sure each person has a partner. You can have three people in a partnership if necessary).
- Review the word of the day. Ask a student to use it correctly in a sentence.

GOAL COMMITMENT—WORKSHEET

LESSON #4

I, _____ understand what commitment is. I know and understand that all that is asked of me is to:

- Learn how to set a goal
- Keep my eyes on that goal
- Start walking

I will commit to learn and follow this Goals Program. I will help my teammates to do this and if I were afraid or fainthearted, I would quit now so I would not block the progress of my teammates.

_____   _____
Accountability Partner   Signature

The accountability partner is the person who will keep you on track. Your partner will encourage you and be there for you when times are difficult.

When geese fly, they fly in a "V" formation. They often look disorganized because they are always changing the lead bird. Wind-tunnel tests show that this is the most effective method of flying. The lead bird takes the brunt of the wind resistance and the others follow in the draft. Because the lead is the most difficult position, they change often so each bird will take his turn leading. Should one of the birds become sick, another will stay with him until he either survives or dies.

An athletic team should be like these geese. Being the leader is the most difficult position, unless it is shared. Every drill, every play, someone should be stepping forward and sharing the leadership. Every bird flies at the front out of loyalty to the team. None stays in the draft all the time. They all take their turn and that is why they are the greatest flying machine. Your accountability partner is the one who stays with you when you are down. He will help you get caught up. It is not his job to baby you, but it is his job to keep you up and keep you going. Each of you should sharpen the other. If you don't have an accountability partner, a coach will volunteer.

Word of the Day: Partnership—a relationship involving close cooperation between parties have specified joint rights and responsibilities

CHARACTERISTICS OF GOALS (PART 1)— COACH'S NOTES

SAY: (5 MINUTES)

You've made the commitment, and you now have an accountability partner. Now it is time to learn the characteristics of goals. If you are going to have them and follow them, you have to know everything about them.

For goals to be effective, they need to be big, because it takes a big goal to create the excitement necessary for accomplishment. No excitement exists with mediocrity. The goal must be big enough to stir your passion. When you picture the end result, you must feel an excitement—an enthusiasm—to get started. A wise man once said, "Make no small plans, for they have no capacity to stir men's souls."

Can goals be too big? Without a doubt—yes. For example, consider the case of a football coach who held a team meeting and asked the players to set a team goal This team said they wanted to be state champions. The problem with this goal was that this particular school had not won a playoff game since 1949! What do you think the chances were of them winning the 5A State Championship? Do you tell them they have little chance, or do you allow them to set a goal that is almost surely unreachable? The coach did the wrong thing: He allowed them to have that goal and it was a negative experience for everyone.

Another football coach took a different approach. Bob Stull, the head football coach at the University of Texas at El Paso, took UTEP to a bowl game for the first time in many years, but it didn't happen overnight.

One of the goals for his first UTEP team was to defensively shut out *one* opponent. This task had not been done at UTEP in many years. Late in a losing season, this goal became huge, because they still had a shot at reaching one of their team goals. They had a spot down the railroad tracks that they could see—and they kept walking.

Did they set a goal to win the national championship? No, they didn't set a goal that, realistically, most of the players, coaches, and alumni couldn't see. They set goals that made them strive. When they got to those spots on the railroad tracks, they found a new spot further down the track and kept walking, right to a winning season and eventually a bowl bid. They set some big goals, but not unrealistic ones.

(*Note*: Use an appropriate example from your sport.) If you are the third-team guard, making All-State is a little unrealistic right now. First, set your sights on being the second-team guard. Just like prize fighters, you must move up one notch at a time, in most cases. If fighters get overzealous and fight someone way above them, they may lose badly and not only lose confidence but begin losing hope as well.

If you bench press 100 pounds and you set a goal of 400 pounds, you are being unrealistic. If you set your goal at 120 pounds and have a plan to get there, 120 is the first step on the way to 400.

A follow-up note on that high school team: They set some more reachable goals the next year. They continued walking toward specific points on the railroad track until they could see further. They kept setting goals. Four years later, they set a realistically big goal to be the state champions—and that is exactly what happened.

Goals must be big enough to create a passion within you and not so big that they are unrealistic. You will be expected to write and complete a goal in the following areas:

- Academic—subjects other than extracurricular
- Physical—strength, speed, or size
- Athletic performance—how well you will perform for the team
- Family, financial, spiritual—any one of the three or another area you choose

Start thinking about what your goals will be and, as you learn the characteristics of well-established goals, start painting a picture of exactly what they will be. Remember that the first characteristic of a goal is that it must be big, but not unrealistic.

The second characteristic of goals is that they should be long-range enough so that you are able to overcome some short-term obstacles. The goal should not be for one week; circumstances may cause such goals to be lost. If your physical goal is to lose 30 pounds, set your target date for at least four months away, meaning that less than 8 pounds must be lost per month. This timeframe allows you room if some emergency circumstances occur.

When a plane leaves the airport, it may get blown off-course; it does not go back to the airport and start over. It corrects the mistake and moves forward. Obstacles will occur as you attempt to reach your goal. You did not call the chief of police this morning and ask when all the lights would be green before you left your house. Stoplights and caution lights mark your journey. You don't quit because you hit a red light. You stop, regroup, and keep going. Other people or circumstances may stop you temporarily, but only you can stop yourself permanently.

Can a goal be too long-range? Yes. Do not procrastinate. You have probably heard your mother say a thousand times, "Do not put off 'til tomorrow what should be done today." You are not going to lose 30 pounds this week, but setting that same goal with a two-year timeframe would be lazy. Set a time line that has some logic behind it. Some goals will have a built-in time line, such as a goal to score 100 percent on your history final. Others require some forethought and planning. A sense of urgency should exist, but not a panic.

Again, your goal should be *big* and *long-range*. You should be thinking about what your goals are going to be and some appropriate time lines. Talk to your friends and parents about ideas. One piece of advice: Share your "give up" goals with everyone. If, for a physical goal, you are going to give up dipping tobacco, tell it to everyone. When giving up something, you will get help from everyone. They will all hold you accountable.

Share your "go up" goals only with people who want to help you "go up." If you want to go up to the top third of your class, tell only those people who believe in you and want to help you. If your "go up" goal is to win a district title, you don't need to tell your opponent. Doing so only provides motivation for them. It gives them a goal. Don't do anything to help your opponents.

DO: (15 MINUTES)

- Lead a discussion of Questions #1–3 on the worksheet.
- Give the students adequate time to write four goals in Question #4. This list is a starting point for these goals.
- Review the word of the day. Ask a student to use it correctly in a sentence.

CHARACTERISTICS OF GOALS (PART 1)— WORKSHEET

"Maturity is the willingness to sacrifice a short-term pleasure for a long-range goal."
—Dennis Parker

For discussion:

1. Why should a goal be big?

   _____

   _____

2. Why should a goal be long-range?

   _____

   _____

3. What are some examples of "give up" goals? What are some examples of "go up" goals?

   _____

   _____

4. Write down one goal in each of these areas:

   Physical: _____

   _____

   Academic: _____

   _____

   Athletic performance: _____

   _____

   Family, financial, or spiritual: _____

   _____

Word of the Day: Maturity—the characteristics associated with an adult

LESSON #6

CHARACTERISTICS OF GOALS (PART 2)— COACH'S NOTES

SAY: (5 MINUTES)

To recap what you have learned in earlier lessons:

- You understand the importance of goals.
- You know the definition of a goal.
- You made the commitment to set goals.
- You know they must be big and long-range.

This lesson covers the last two characteristics of goals. Goals must be worked on daily. Charlie Cullen expressed this concept best when he said, "The opportunity does not come cascading down like a torrential Niagara Falls, but rather it comes slowly, one day at a time." You may have heard the saying, "By the mile it's a trial, by the inch it's a cinch."

Jerry Trees was a great track coach. Each year, he would set a goal for where each of his weight men should be by the district meet. But he would post each Monday only what he expected them to throw at that week's meet. By the district meet, he was almost exactly right in terms of where each athlete stood. He gave them a spot on the railroad track that they could see and then gave them another one a little farther down the track. He would not give them the district-meet goal, instead providing goals for only one week at a time.

This process works in every field. Daily objectives are absolutely necessary to reach a goal. Years ago, a company paid a consultant $35,000 for an idea that made their company more productive. The idea: Each employee wrote six objectives that he was going to get done before he left that day. What caused the increased productivity? Simple: It literally forced every employee not to be stagnant. They could not confuse activity with accomplishment. No matter how busy they appeared, they had to be results-oriented. They had six objectives to meet each day. They had immediate feedback on the success of the day. By taking care of the daily objectives, they moved closer to the goal and closer to the end result.

Remember, Maxwell Maltz said that man functions like a bicycle. You keep your balance by moving forward. You cannot stand still. If you move forward just slightly each day, you are getting closer to your goal. It is important that you prepare to keep a daily record, a daily grade on how you are doing on your four goals. At the beginning of every day you will give yourself a grade on how you did the day before on each goal. If you moved forward, you will give yourself a plus (+); if you did not move forward, you will give yourself a minus (-). You are responsible to reach your ultimate goal and the daily goals will keep you accountable.

The fourth characteristic of goals is that they must be specific. On the hottest day of the year, get the most powerful magnifying glass you can buy in a store and a box of newspaper clippings. Even though you magnify the power of the sun through the glass, you will never start a fire if you keep the glass moving. However, if you hold the glass still, and focus it on the paper, you harness the power of the sun and multiply it through the glass. Then you can start a roaring fire.

No matter how much power, brilliance, or energy you have, if you don't harness it and focus it on a specific target, you're never going to accomplish as much as your ability warrants. The hunter who brings back the birds doesn't shoot the covey. He selects one quail as a specific target.

The art of goal-setting is to focus on one specific, detailed objective. Doing "my best" is an easy out. That type of goal is completely nonspecific and holds no accountability. Making All-District or All-State is not specific enough. To accomplish this goal, you depend on your coach to nominate you and the other coaches to vote for you. Consider this alternative:

(*Note*: Use specific examples from your sport.) If your performance goal was to make 14 unassisted tackles on the average, do you think you would make All-District? What if you completed 75 percent of your passes? Graded 80 percent with three pancake blocks?

Get the picture?

DO: (15 MINUTES)

- Discuss the questions found on the worksheet.
- Give the students time to rewrite any goal so that they are specific, big, and long-range.
- Review the word of the day. Ask a student to use it correctly in a sentence.

CHARACTERISTICS OF GOALS (PART 2)— WORKSHEET

"The goals you set must be challenging. At the same time, they should be realistic and attainable, not impossible to reach. They should be challenging enough to make you stretch, but not so far you break."

—Rick Hanson

For discussion:

1. Why are daily objectives necessary to reach a long-range goal?

   _____

   _____

   _____

   _____

2. Why is it important that you set goals that are specific?

   _____

   _____

   _____

   _____

3. Look at each of the four goals you wrote in Lesson #5 and ask yourself: Are they big? Long-range? Specific? Can they be broken down into a daily objective? Rework any goals so they fit the four characteristics of goals.

   _____

   _____

   _____

   _____

Word of the Day: Accountability—an obligation or willingness to accept responsibility or to account for one's actions

BECOMING A FLEA TRAINER—COACH'S NOTES

SAY: (5 MINUTES)

It is important that you understand how your mind and body work to reach a goal. When you commit a specific goal to your mind, your success instinct immediately begins to work to take you to that picture. Whatever you paint as an end result, your success instinct will begin to take you there.

Consider the following story of two golfers: The first "sees" the ball landing on the green. The second takes out two balls because he "knows" one will go in the water hazard. What do you think is the final result of each golfer's shot? Which has a success instinct and which has a failure instinct?

You do not need to concern yourself with how to get to the goal. Concern yourself with the picture and the means will take care of themselves. Your body cannot tell the difference between a real experience and one that is vividly imagined. This concept is the key to reaching a destination to which we have never been.

It may surprise you to learn that you will never have success until you learn to train fleas. You train fleas by putting them in a jar with a top on it. The fleas will jump up and hit the top over and over again. As you watch them jump and hit the top, you will notice something interesting. The fleas continue to jump, but they no longer jump high enough to hit the top. Then—and this is true—you can take the top off and, though the fleas continue to jump, they won't jump out of the jar. They won't jump out because they have conditioned themselves to jump just so high and that's all they can do.

People are the same way. You may start out in life planning to write a book, climb a mountain, break a record, or make a contribution. Initially, your dreams and ambitions have no limits, but along the roadway of life you bump your head and stub your toe a few times. At this point, your "friends" and associates often make negative comments about life in general and about you in particular. As a result, you become a SNIOP—a person who is Susceptible to the Negative Influences of Other People. This phenomenon is another reason why it is important to be careful about who you show your "go up" goals to.

The most outstanding example of a flea trainer is Roger Bannister. For years, athletes tried to run a mile in less than four minutes. The barrier seemed unbreakable. Doctors even told athletes that the heart would explode if they ran the mile in under four minutes. The general consensus was that the sub-four-minute mile was beyond the physical capacity of the human being.

Roger Bannister wouldn't be "SNIOPed." He trained hard. He imagined himself breaking the four-minute barrier. He broke the mile down into laps and hired four men to pace him each lap. He knew exactly how many strides he took per lap. He broke the four-minute barrier. Less than six weeks later, John Landy of Australia accomplished the same feat. All of a sudden, athletes all over the world were running the mile in under four minutes. The four-minute barrier was broken because it was mental and not physical.

In case you missed the point, a flea trainer is a person who jumps out of the jar. He's driven from within and is not "SNIOPed" by negative influences. Once you set the goal, your success instinct will begin working on it. Develop the picture of what you want and do not listen to the SNIOPs of the world.

DO: (15 MINUTES)

- Read aloud the flea trainer certificate and have the students fill in their names.
- Lead a discussion of the questions found on the student worksheet.
- Review the word of the day. Ask a student to use it correctly in a sentence.

Let the whole world know that _____ is a fully qualified, dedicated "flea trainer." By jumping out of the jar, you are earning the rights and privileges this world has to offer.

Flea trainers are people who are driven from within and are not SNIOPS (susceptible to negative influences of other people). They have removed their own ceilings and are teaching others to do the same.

Flea trainers work at seeing people through, instead of seeing through people. They teach others how to "get on" instead of telling them where to "get off." They are confident, but not arrogant, and they know how to serve without being servile.

Flea trainers seek "total" success and a well-balanced life by building on honesty, love, character, loyalty, faith, and integrity. They know that a dedicated effort is its own reward and that what you get by reaching your objective is not as important as what you become by reaching that objective.

You are going up with the knowledge that "he climbs highest who helps another up."

_____   _____
Accountability Partner   Flea Trainer

BECOMING A FLEA TRAINER—WORKSHEET

"You need to overcome the tug of people against you as you reach for high goals."
—General George S. Patton

For discussion:

1. Think of an example of when you let other people tell you that you couldn't accomplish something and you believed them (you were SNIOPed), and share the story with the group. What did you learn from that experience?

_____

_____

_____

_____

_____

_____

2. How can you help others "jump out of the jar" and see past self-imposed limitations?

_____

_____

_____

_____

_____

_____

_____

Word of the Day: Influence—to affect or alter by indirect or intangible means; can be positive or negative

USING TIME WISELY—COACH'S NOTES

LESSON #8

SAY: (5 MINUTES)

You've learned what a goal is—a vision with work. And you understand the importance of goals and know their characteristics:

- Big
- Long-range
- Checked daily
- Specific

You know that you have a success instinct and that when you put the goal picture in your mind your subconscious starts working on it immediately. You have been thinking about the four goals you are going to work on in each of the four areas:

- Physical
- Academic
- Athletic performance
- Family, financial, or spiritual

It is now time to begin the "journey." Goal-setting is simply a journey in which you set a destination and begin working to get to that point.

The first thing you have to determine is where you are. If you are going somewhere, you have to know your beginning point. Write down everything you did yesterday and the time you spent doing it. Be specific. Do not simply write "English." Write briefly and specifically about exactly what you accomplished in English class. For time you spent doing nothing organized, write "free time." What you are going to learn is that you have time you are wasting, and that organization can be used to your benefit. Instead of "killing time," make your time count for you.

Every person has 24 hours a day, 7 days a week, 365 days a year. Successful people do not necessarily work harder than others. They work smarter. As you write your daily time log, be alert to see where you will be able to schedule time to work on goals.

The true mark of commitment is how your time is spent. If a man invests little, he expects little or no profit. What you put in is what you get out. For example, if you invest $0.25 in General Motors and you learn that General Motors may be facing bankruptcy, your attitude is, "So what, it is only a quarter." On the other hand, if you have saved every penny you have earned from an after-school and weekend job, if you have denied yourself a car and parties to invest your savings in General Motors and then hear that General Motors is facing bankruptcy and that you will possibly lose all your money, your attitude is "No way! I may have to reorganize or change, but we are not going bankrupt!"

Goal-getting works the same way. When you invest the time and commitment to get to that point, you will make the effort to reach the goal. If your team goal is to win the game, and you have put in the time and effort and the other team is about to score, your response is, "They will not score. I have invested too much to give up now!"

You might say this is paying the price to be successful. But try to look at it another way. You pay a price to be a failure. You all spend time. Some spend it wisely doing the things that will make them successful. Others spend it foolishly and wonder where it went. Fielding Yost expressed this concept best when he said, "To me no coach in America asks a man to make any sacrifice. He requests that he do the opposite: think clean…live clean…come clean. He requests that he stop doing all the things that destroy him physically, mentally, and morally and begin doing all the things that make him finer, keener, and more confident. Athletics is a privilege, a luxury, but never a sacrifice."

The sacrifice is made by cigarette smokers. The smoker sacrifices 14 minutes of his life every time he smokes a cigarette.

The sacrifice is made by overweight people. They sacrifice hours of enjoyment because they are too tired from carrying the extra weight to really enjoy the day.

The sacrifice is made by the "cool" guy. He is afraid to love and give of himself, so he never turns loose and gives his all. In life, he receives only what he has given—little.

The sacrifice is made by the weak athlete. He never knows what it is like to use strength as his ally.

The sacrifice is made by the athlete who does not set goals and discipline himself to follow a plan. He wanders aimlessly along, blown by the winds of time. He never accomplishes.

Once you realize that you are not paying a price, and that you are instead enjoying the benefits, you can determine where you want to go. But first, you've got to know where your time is being spent.

DO: (15 MINUTES)

- Give each student adequate time to fill in the schedule. (If yesterday was not an average day, have them guess what an "average" school day is like.)
- Ask the following questions:
  ✓ What did you learn about how your time was spent?
  ✓ What do you need to change to have time to work on your goals?
- Review the word of the day. Ask a student to use it correctly in a sentence.

USING TIME WISELY—WORKSHEET

"Do not squander time, for that is the stuff life is made of."

—Benjamin Franklin

Fill in the schedule below using yesterday—or an "average" school day if yesterday was not typical. Be specific in what you did and what you accomplished during each hour. If you were not doing anything specific, write in "free time."

6:00 am _____

7:00 am _____

8:00 am _____

9:00 am _____

10:00 am _____

11:00 am _____

12:00 pm _____

1:00 pm _____

2:00 pm _____

3:00 pm _____

4:00 pm _____

5:00 pm _____

6:00 pm _____

7:00 pm _____

8:00 pm _____

9:00 pm _____

10:00 pm _____

11:00 pm _____

12:00 am _____

Word of the Day: Invest—to commit in order to earn a return

PHYSICAL GOAL—COACH'S NOTES

SAY: (5 MINUTES)

You now know your starting point. A goal is a journey. You started by seeing where you were. Now set the destination of where you want to go. This lesson will begin with the physical goal. Ask yourself the following questions:

- Physically, where do you want to go? Your goal must be big, specific, long-range, and have daily objectives.
- Why do you want to go? This question is the most important of all. You must tune in to radio station WII-FM, which stands for What's In It For Me. This physical goal has to be so important to you that it stirs a passion within you. When you write down the benefits of reaching this goal, it must excite you. If it is not important, if it does not excite you, chances are that you will not be successful. When asked on his deathbed what was the key to success, the great scientist Ivan Pavlov replied, "Passion and gradualness." You must have a passion, a burning desire to get where you want to go, and you must be willing to do it gradually.
- When do you want to get there? Your response must be very specific. It cannot be "next year" or "this fall." A specific date is needed.
- When do you start? Tomorrow is the greatest labor-saving device in the country. You cannot put off the beginning date. A sign reads, "Free Soda Pop Tomorrow." The only problem is tomorrow never comes. Today should be the starting date, unless special circumstances exist.
- What does it cost? No one begins a journey without first deciding if they can afford it. Figure out what the obstacles are that you must defeat to get to the goal. The minute you write down the obstacle and decide you want to overcome it, the success instinct in you will begin searching for answers.
- How do you get there? You know where you want to go and when you want to get there, and have a plan to overcome the obstacles. Now, map out the route you will take to get there. Daily objectives come into play at this point. You must grade yourself daily, with a plus or minus. Did you follow the plan to get closer to the goal? If yes, put a plus (+) in your notebook. If not, put a minus (-). Do not get down on yourself if every day is not a plus. Some days will be a minus, but those setbacks are temporary. Keep pushing until there are more plusses.
- Who is responsible? If you are depending on someone else, or if you are counting on luck, you will not have a chance to succeed. You are responsible in spite of circumstances. Do not allow temporary setbacks to prevent you from getting to where you want to go.

It is important to note that private achievement precedes public achievement. Public achievement is having your perfect test score announced by your teacher. Before that can happen, you must spend nights in private achieving the knowledge necessary to know the answers. Public achievement is winning in a big game. For this to happen, you must have spent time conditioning and working in private. Walter Payton ran for more than 12,000 yards in public. Beforehand, Walter Payton ran many more than 12,000 yards in private, preparing himself.

In his book, *See You at the Top*, Zig Ziglar explains how, by using this goals formula, he lost 37 pounds in 10 months.

- Where did he want to go? From 202 pounds down to 165 pounds
- Why did he want to go? For health reasons, longer life, better quality of life, and to heed his own advice
- When did he want to get there? In 10 months
- When did he start? That very day
- What did it cost? For Ziglar, this goal meant working good nutrition and fitness into an irregular schedule that forced him to eat late at night. It cost him his love of sweets. It meant beginning an exercise program.
- How did he get there? He scheduled his workout around his speaking, ate nutritious late-night snacks, cut out fried foods, ate only at the table, ate slowly, ate sweets only on Sunday, and started an exercise program that began with jogging one block and built up to several miles
- Who accepted the responsibility? He did

Arriving home from a trip at 4:30 in the morning, Ziglar refused to take the morning off, got up at 5:30 and jogged. He did not make an exception. An exception is the single most detrimental factor to reaching goals. Do not make exceptions.

DO: (15 MINUTES)

- Have each student set a physical goal using the worksheet as a guide. (They began this process in Lesson #5. Be sure they are writing realistic, specific goals.)
- Ask for volunteers to share their goals.
- Review the word of the day. Ask a student to use it correctly in a sentence.

PHYSICAL GOAL—WORKSHEET

"The successful man lengthens his stride when he discovers that the signpost has deceived him; the failure looks for a place to sit down."

—J.R. Rogers

For discussion:

1. Where do you want to go? (Specifically write down your goal.)

   _____

2. Why do you want to go? (What are the benefits to you?)

   _____

   _____

   _____

3. When do you want to get there? (Choose a specific date.)

   _____

4. When do you start?

   _____

5. What does it cost? (List the obstacles standing between you and this goal.)

   _____

   _____

6. How do you get there? (Develop a plan of action.)

   _____

   _____

7. Who is responsible?

   _____

Word of the Day: Exception—a case to which a rule does not apply

ACADEMIC GOAL—COACH'S NOTES

SAY: (5 MINUTES)

With this lesson, you are going to begin grading yourselves on your goals. Did you do what you needed to do yesterday on your physical goal? If yes, congratulations! You have taken the first step. If you answered no, recommit yourself to start today. Ask yourself: What got in my way? How can I tackle that obstacle?

DO: (15 MINUTES)

- Give students a chance to grade themselves on their physical goals. Discuss their progress.
- Have each student set an academic goal using the same process as in Lesson #9.
- Ask for volunteers to share their goals.
- Review the word of the day. Ask a student to use it correctly in a sentence.

ACADEMIC GOAL—WORKSHEET

For discussion:

1. Where do you want to go? (Specifically write down your goal.)

   _____

2. Why do you want to go? (What are the benefits to you?)

   _____

   _____

3. When do you want to get here? (Choose a specific date.)

   _____

4. When do you start?

   _____

5. What does it cost? (List the obstacles standing between you and this goal.)

   _____

   _____

6. How do you get there? (Develop a plan of action.)

   _____

   _____

   _____

7. Who is responsible?

   _____

Word of the Day: Stepwise—marked by or proceeding in steps

ATHLETIC GOAL—COACH'S NOTES

SAY: (5 MINUTES)

With this lesson, you are going to continue grading yourselves on your goals. Did you do what you needed to do yesterday on your academic goal? If yes, congratulations! You have taken the first step. If you answered no, recommit yourself to start today. Ask yourself: What got in my way? How can I tackle that obstacle?

DO: (15 MINUTES)

- Give students a chance to grade themselves on their physical and academic goals. Discuss their progress.
- Have each student set an athletic goal using the same process as in Lessons #9 and #10.
- Ask for volunteers to share their goals.
- Review the word of the day. Ask a student to use it correctly in a sentence.

ATHLETIC GOAL—WORKSHEET

"In life, as in football, you won't go far unless you know where the goalposts are."
—Arnold Glasgow

For discussion:

1. Where do you want to go? (Specifically write down your goal.)

_____

2. Why do you want to go? (What are the benefits to you?)

_____

_____

3. When do you want to get here? (Choose a specific date.)

_____

4. When do you start?

_____

5. What does it cost? (List the obstacles standing between you and this goal.)

_____

_____

6. How do you get there? (Develop a plan of action.)

_____

_____

_____

7. Who is responsible?

_____

Word of the Day: Obstacle—something that impedes progress or achievement

PERSONAL GOAL—COACH'S NOTES

LESSON #12

SAY: (5 MINUTES)

With this lesson, you are going to continue grading yourselves on your goals. Did you do what you needed to do yesterday on your athletic goal? If yes, congratulations! You have taken the first step. If you answered no, recommit yourself to start today. Ask yourself: What got in my way? How can I tackle that obstacle?

DO: (15 MINUTES)

*   Give students a chance to grade themselves on their physical, academic, and athletic goals. Discuss their progress.
*   Have each student set a personal goal using the same process as in Lessons #9, #10, and #11.
*   Ask for volunteers to share their goals.
*   Review the word of the day. Ask a student to use it correctly in a sentence.

Photo Credit: Gavin Barker/Touchline Photo

PERSONAL GOAL—WORKSHEET

"What you get by achieving your goals is not as important as what you have become by achieving your goals."

—Zig Ziglar

For discussion:

1. Where do you want to go? (Specifically write down your goal.)

    _____

2. Why do you want to go? (What are the benefits to you?)

    _____

    _____

3. When do you want to get here? (Choose a specific date.)

    _____

4. When do you start?

    _____

5. What does it cost? (List the obstacles standing between you and this goal.)

    _____

    _____

6. How do you get there? (Develop a plan of action.)

    _____

    _____

7. Who is responsible?

    _____

Word of the Day: Attain—to succeed in a directed effort, process, or progression

DAILY GRADE (PART 1)—COACH'S NOTES

SAY: (5 MINUTES)

This lesson allows you to discuss the progress you are making on your four goals. Now is the time to remember the importance of discipline. You must "keep on keeping on" for the goals to become a reality. You want these daily objectives to become habits for you.

Listen to the following story and see if you can guess what I am talking about: "I am your constant companion. I am your greatest helper or heaviest burden. I will push you onward and upward or drag you down to failure. I am completely at your command. Ninety percent of the things you do might just as well be turned over to me, and I will be able to do them quickly and correctly. I am easily managed. Show me exactly how you want something done and after a few lessons I will do them automatically. I am the servant of all great people and, alas, of all the failures as well. I am not a machine, though I work with all the precision of a machine, plus the intelligence of a man. You can run me for profit or run me for ruin—it makes no difference to me. Take me, train me, be firm with me, and I will place the world at your feet. Be easy with me and I will destroy you. Who am I? I am Habit."

—Author Unknown

All bad habits start slowly and gradually build until, before you realize you've got the habit, the habit has you. Examples are obesity, promiscuity, drug and alcohol addiction, pornography, and tardiness. No one gains a hundred extra pounds in a week. They add it on "one more bite" at a time. Alcohol and drug addiction follow the same pattern, as do thievery, immorality, and other vices. On the other hand, good habits must be grabbed firmly, forcefully, and with a strong commitment. That decision, reinforced by your will to take action on your commitment, regardless of how you feel at the moment, will produce in an amazingly short period of time some incredible results.

DO: (15 MINUTES)

- Lead a discussion from the questions on the student worksheet. Be sure to let the students do the talking and always ask for specific examples.
- Discuss progress made on the goals.
- Review the word of the day. Ask a student to use it correctly in a sentence.

DAILY GRADE (PART 1)—WORKSHEET

LESSON #13

"If I do not practice one day, I know it. If I do not practice the next day, the orchestra knows it. If I do not practice the third day, the whole world knows it."

—Ignacy Paderewski, Polish pianist

For discussion:

1. What habits do you have that positively affect your ability to reach your goals?

_____

_____

_____

_____

2. What habits do you have that negatively affect your ability to reach your goals?

_____

_____

_____

_____

3. Review your responses to Question #2. How do you intend to break those habits? Be specific.

_____

_____

_____

_____

Word of the Day: Commitment—an agreement or pledge to do something in the future

DAILY GRADE (PART 2)—COACH'S NOTES

LESSON #14

SAY: (5 MINUTES)

This lesson continues the discussion you have been having about your four goals. Take some time to think about what your experiences so far have taught you about how to set goals for yourself. It is important that you understand that it is okay to make adjustments to your goals—as long as you are not making excuses and unnecessarily extending your time lines or lessening your commitment to this process. Proper adjustments may include shortening the length of a long-term goal if you're progressing more quickly than you expected or altering the extent of change if your original goal is proving unrealistic. You will get better at setting and adhering to goals as you learn more about yourself.

DO (20 MINUTES)

- Discuss progress made on the four goals.
- Lead a discussion from the questions on the student worksheet. Be sure to let the students do the talking and always ask for specific examples.
- Review the word of the day. Ask a student to use it correctly in a sentence.

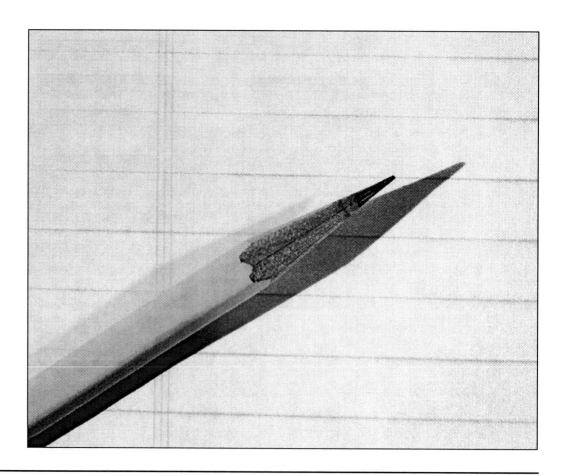

DAILY GRADE (PART 2)—WORKSHEET

"Success is a journey—not a destination."

—H. Tom Collard

For discussion:

1. What have you learned about yourself during the first steps of working toward your goals?

    _____

    _____

    _____

    _____

2. Which of the four categories has been the easiest for you? Why do you think that is?

    _____

    _____

    _____

    _____

3. Which of the four categories has been the most difficult? Why do you think that is?

    _____

    _____

    _____

    _____

Word of the Day: Journey—travel or passage from one place to another; something suggesting travel or passage (i.e., from youth to maturity)

DAILY GRADE (PART 3)—COACH'S NOTES

LESSON #15

SAY: (5 MINUTES)

Again, this lesson continues your discussion of the four goals you have been working toward. Two of the questions you were asked in Lesson #14 addressed how easy or difficult you were finding each category. Remember, the four goal categories are physical, academic, athletic, and personal. As athletes, many of you may find that the physical and athletic goals are the most fun to work on, while the academic and personal goals may be more of a struggle. For others, the opposite may be true. What do you think? Spend some time thinking about your response to this question and what it says about you as a student, an athlete, and a person. Do you think you may be in need of a priority shift?

DO: (20 MINUTES)

- Discuss progress made on the four goals.
- Lead a discussion from the questions on the student worksheet. Be sure to let the students do the talking and always ask for specific examples.
- Review the word of the day. Ask a student to use it correctly in a sentence.

DAILY GRADE (PART 3)—WORKSHEET

"To believe a thing impossible is to make it so."

—French proverb

For discussion:

1. List the four goal categories—physical, academic, athletic, and personal—in order of importance to you. How has the order of that list changed over the course of this curriculum?

_____

_____

_____

_____

2. How do you think the order of that list will change at various stages of your life—one year from now, 10 years from now, 20 years from now?

_____

_____

_____

_____

_____

_____

_____

_____

Word of the Day: Pessimism—a tendency to take the least hopeful view of a situation or to anticipate the worst

CARPE DIEM—COACH'S NOTES

SAY: (5 MINUTES)

The term *carpe diem*—which means seize the day—was coined by a man named Horace in 35 B.C. This term was referenced in Dead Poet's Society, a movie starring Robin Williams. In the movie, Williams is an English teacher who teaches his students how to seize the day. John Wooden says to make each day your masterpiece. What you do today will probably have a great deal of influence on what will happen tomorrow. Make this day your very best.

A teacher once asked her students how many of them liked ice cream. All the children raised their hands. The teacher then said whoever had ice cream on a daily basis could drop their hands. A few dropped their hands. The teacher then said those who had ice cream once a week could drop their hands. A few more hands dropped. Finally, the teacher asked how many students had ice cream once a year. Every hand dropped except for one little boy. He was so excited and enthusiastic. The teacher asked him if he loved ice cream. "Yes, ma'am," he said. The teacher asked him how often he ate ice cream. "Once a year," he said with an excitement that only a youngster could have. Perplexed, the teacher asked him why he was so happy. The boy replied, "Today is the day!" Try to look at everything in that way. *Carpe diem*…today *is* the day.

DO: (15 MINUTES)

- Lead a discussion from the questions on the student worksheet. Be sure to let the students do the talking and always ask for specific examples.
- Review the word of the day. Ask a student to use it correctly in a sentence.

CARPE DIEM—WORKSHEET

"Life is divided into three terms—that which was, which is, and which will be. Let us learn from the past to profit by the present and from the present to live better for the future."

—William Wordsworth

For discussion:

1. What can you do about yesterday?

_____

_____

_____

2. What you do today affects tomorrow. How?

_____

_____

_____

3. What is wrong with living in the past or living in the future?

_____

_____

_____

4. List some ways you can get yourself excited and motivated about each and every day. (How do you persuade yourself to look at every day as "the day you get ice cream?")

_____

_____

_____

Word of the Day: Seize—to take possession of

KEEP YOUR GOALS IN SIGHT—COACH'S NOTES

SAY: (5 MINUTES)

When she looked ahead, Florence Chadwick saw nothing but a solid wall of fog. Her body was numb. She had been swimming for nearly 16 hours. She already was the first woman to swim the English Channel in both directions. Now, at age 34, her goal was to become the first woman to swim from Catalina Island to the California coast.

On that Fourth of July morning in 1952, the sea was like an ice bath and the fog was so dense that she could hardly see her support boats. Sharks cruised toward her lone figure, only to be driven away by rifle shots. Against the frigid grip of the sea, she struggled on—hour after hour—while the nation watched on television.

Alongside Florence in one of the boats, her mother and her trainer offered encouragement. They told her it wasn't much farther, but all she could see was fog. They urged her not to quit. She never had…until then. With only half a mile to go, she asked to be pulled out.

Still thawing her chilled body several hours later, she told a reporter, "Look, I'm not excusing myself, but if I could have seen land I might have made it." It was not fatigue or even the cold water that defeated her. It was the fog. She was unable to see her goal.

Two months later, she tried again. This time, despite the same dense fog, she swam with her faith intact and her goal clearly pictured in her mind. She knew that somewhere behind that fog was land and this time she made it. Florence Chadwick became the first woman to swim the Catalina Channel, eclipsing the men's record by two hours.

DO: (15 MINUTES)

- Lead a discussion from the questions on the student worksheet. Be sure to let the students do the talking and always ask for specific examples.
- Review the word of the day. Ask a student to use it correctly in a sentence.

KEEP YOUR GOALS IN SIGHT—WORKSHEET

"I can't believe that God put us on this earth to be ordinary."

—Lou Holtz

For discussion:

1. Write about a time in your life when a "wall of fog" kept you from your goals.

   _____

   _____

   _____

   _____

2. What could you have done to help the fog lift?

   _____

   _____

   _____

   _____

3. Do you think someone in your life could talk you through a situation like the one Florence Chadwick faced—that is, support you when you can no longer see your goal or when your goal seems out of reach? Are you that person for someone else?

   _____

   _____

   _____

   _____

Word of the Day: Encourage—to fill with courage or strength of purpose

On the following pages is a speech by Bob Stull, given when he was head football coach at the University of Texas at El Paso. It is probably the best speech you will ever hear or read on the topic of team goals.

Changing Attitudes...Winning

I want to thank Jim Walden for the opportunity to speak at this convention. It is a great honor to be invited to speak at the AFCA Clinic and I want to recognize my staff, Dirk Koetter, Kevin Faulkner, Andy Reid, Mike Ward, and Larry Hoefer on offense, and Mike Church, Steve Telander, Mo Latimore, and Ned Maypole on defense, for helping make this opportunity possible. Before I talk about changing attitudes, I feel it is important everyone understands that in order to change an attitude you have to understand the existing one.

The number one question that the news media asked me when I was hired at UTEP was, "Why would you take a job that is traditionally a graveyard for coaches?" My wife commented on the question by saying, "You know, that sounds so final." I had never thought of it that way, but I had to agree. Since 1974 UTEP had never won more than two games and hadn't had a winning season in almost 20 years! Whenever I would speak at a service club or university function, someone would always pull me aside after my talk and say, "Just beat New Mexico State and two other teams and they'll elect you mayor and build you a monument in the center of town."

The first year we did beat New Mexico State and three other teams, but I was disappointed to find out there was no strong movement in either direction. However, this year, before our BYU game, when we were 5-1 in conference play and still in the conference race, "Bob Stull for Mayor" T-shirts went on sale for $15.00 at a local restaurant. However, after the game, which we lost, prices were reduced to $1.25. You know what our relatives got for Christmas!

As you can see, the people of El Paso were starved for a competitive football team. Fortunately, we have over 500,000 people in El Paso with no competition for the entertainment dollar other than high school athletics. We have no professional team or local college to compete with. This was a factor when I took the job because there was a potential for an increase in attendance. Obviously, this would mean more money for our Athletics Program. The city was a great backer of our basketball team, averaging over 12,000 at home games. Of course, Don Haskins has been extremely successful over the years, including over 500 victories, five back-to-back WAC titles, and a national championship in 1966. However, because of the basketball support, I felt if we could become competitive, people would support us also in football. Fortunately, I was right on that point, because our attendance jumped form 19,000 in 1985, to 27,000 our first year, and just under 43,000 in 1987. But previous to this year, I think the general attitude of the community towards UTEP football was one of apathy. Although they would like to have seen a winning football program, the records were so poor that most

UTEP fans would watch the first few games and then start talking about basketball. The attitude of the players was basically one of a lack of confidence and poor self-esteem stemming from numerous embarrassing and frustrating situations.

Setting Goals

The first step toward developing the proper attitude was developing "a sense of mission"; to become focused on what we wanted to do; to have a clear vision of the team they wanted to become and what we wanted to accomplish. Of course, we had our weekly offensive goals, defensive goals, kicking goals, etc., but we had to set some team goals. It is extremely important to set worthy, but reachable, goals for the team. My first year as head coach at UMass, I made the mistake of setting a goal of simply winning the championship. After losing our first two conference games, I spent the rest of the season trying to find ways to motivate our team. So in looking at UTEP my first year, I felt it would be ridiculous to make winning the WAC Championship our primary goal.

However, I felt that becoming the most improved team in our league would be something we had a chance to accomplish. Since UTEP had not won more than two games since 1974 and hadn't had a winning season since 1970, we had an opportunity to set up a goal chart with plenty of intermediate goals. The great thing about our goal chart the first year was if we won just three games we would be the best team at UTEP in 14 years. Believe me, this kept us going, because after winning two of our first three games we lost seven in a row before winning our last two. No matter how bad things appeared during that period of time, we still knew we could be the best team in years if we could just win one more. This helped keep things in perspective. Here is how we structured our goals the first year.

Level 6	Long-range	Conference champs, bowl game, national ranking
Level 5	Long-range	6 wins, winning season, best since 1967
Level 4	Intermediate	4 conference wins
Level 3	Intermediate	5 wins, most since 1971
Level 2	Primary	3 conference wins, most since 1971
Level 1	Primary	New Mexico State, 1 win

This past year we restructured our goal charts, trying to build on our limited success in 1986. Unlike most teams, each one of our victories last year broke some sort of record dating back five to 20 years. In fact, some things on our chart had never been accomplished. The key here, though, is we set up some measurables. We would review our team goals in our Monday and Thursday team meetings. We also kept a chart listing our accomplishments—WAC Player of the Week, etc. It is a good idea to reinforce positive performance. Here is our goal chart for 1987.

Level 10	Long-range	National ranking
Level 9	Long-range	Bowl game
Level 8	Long-range	Conference champs
Level 7	Intermediate	Most improved team, winning season, 7 wins
Level 6	Intermediate	5 conference wins
Level 5	Intermediate	6 wins, most since 1970
Level 4	Intermediate	4 conference wins; 5 total wins, most since 1971
Level 3	Intermediate	3 conference wins; 4 total wins, most since 1974
Level 2	Intermediate	2 conference wins; 3 total wins, most since 1975
Level 1	Primary	1 win

Taking Responsibility

We sell our players on responsibility. We want our players to understand that they are 100 percent responsible for everything that happens to them, both on and off the field. Winners move forward, while losers make excuses. We do not want our players to blame others for what happens to them. We demand that our players accept total responsibility for their lives. I don't want to hear after a game about the wind, the referees, or any other excuse if we lose a game or don't play well. Each player is held accountable for his particular role in our game plan. If a player is on the offensive unit and also the punt team, he is responsible for understanding our game plan for both, as well as his performance on both. Another player may be only a backup on the kickoff team, but if that is his job he should understand who he would replace in case of an injury, as well as have a complete knowledge of our game plan on our kickoffs. Also, we emphasize that if they don't like their position on our team, if they aren't happy with the way things are going, it's up to them to take the responsibility to change it. And if they can't change it, the least they can do is not complain about it.

Building Confidence

One element our team lacked and we worked hard at developing was confidence. Joe Paterno last year stated that confidence separates winners from losers. I define confidence as the ability to separate a performance from your self-worth. We talked a lot about being able to rebound from a single poor play, or even a poor game. The ability to say, "I'm better than that, that's not like me," rather than the typical negative self-talk, telling yourself how bad you think you are because of what has happened. Being able to maintain confidence when things aren't going right and the crowd is on you is hard to do. Unfortunately, the only way anyone develops confidence is from having positive experiences. But handling your players correctly until you have these positive experiences is important.

In dealing with my coaches, I made sure they understood that developing our team was not going to be easy. In fact, there were probably going to be some very frustrating times ahead. However, what would be important is that we were sound in what we were trying to do, and that we were getting better each week. I wanted our coaches to look for and emphasize the good performances in practice and in games rather than emphasizing our mistakes.

This is especially true with learners. In an established program, we're talking about everyone. We try to encourage progress, as good performance is the accumulation of approximately-rights. Yelling and screaming at players who do not understand exactly what you want will discourage and frustrate them. Don't expect to tell a player how poor he is all week and then expect him to do well in a game. Another important point along these lines is to make sure you tell the player exactly what you want him to do rather than what not to do (a negative of an idea). How many times do we find ourselves telling a player something like "don't' go out of bounds," rather than "stay in bounds and keep the clock moving"? If you tell a player not to do something, studies say you are actually setting him up to do it.

This is because your mind works in pictures and does not recognize the word "don't" from "do." When you approach a water hazard when playing golf and you are thinking, "I can't hit this ball in the water," chances are that's what you are going to do. So when trying to develop confidence in your players, tell them exactly what you want of them in positive terms, and then praise their progress as they become closer to the correct technique or performance you desire.

Overcoming Fear of Failure

One thing that is truly indicative of a team or an individual who hasn't had success is the fear of failure. Our players were more concerned about being involved in a play where the game was lost than being in the paper for making the play that won the game. There is a big difference in thinking here. One who hates to lose but is not afraid to lose will prepare hard and compete equally as hard to win. At times, such a person will also take necessary risks to get the job done. Someone who is afraid to lose, on the other hand, will also prepare hard, but when he is on a critical play he will either play over-cautiously, or overtrain and try too hard, which usually ends with the same disastrous results. How many times have you seen a team blitz in a critical situation, only to have the quarterback complete an easy 12-yard out route? Undoubtedly, the corner has been told to tighten up on the receiver, but his fear of "you can't be beat deep" has caused him to play cautiously.

There is a simple story that illustrates this. Take a 20-foot plank, six inches wide and lay it on the floor. At the end of the plank, put a 10-dollar bill. Now ask a friend to walk along this plank and pick up the 10-dollar bill. You would have no problem getting a volunteer—relatively low risk and high reward. Your friend would probably walk briskly across one foot after the other, and quickly pick up the money. But now take that same 20-foot plank and stretch it between two 30-story buildings. Now ask your friend to perform the exact same task for the same amount of money. Do you think he'd do it? Not on your life. He may shimmy across for $1,000, but if he attempted to walk across his legs would tighten and each step would be painfully slow and wobbly. All of a sudden a new element has entered the performance. Thirty stories of "or else." The fear of failure has made this previously easy task almost impossible. In a game, similar fears of "or else" make the simple techniques you have practiced extremely hard to perform in critical situations.

To help overcome this fear of failure, we told our players that errors are going to happen in a game. Rarely will anyone go through a game without making a mistake. The important thing is for the player to know that he will not be persecuted for making a mistake or being beaten physically as long as he is doing the best he can do with what we have taught him. If something goes wrong, don't panic! Keep your concentration and continue with the techniques and assignments as you were taught. This goes back to confidence, separating one play from your overall performance. Of course, minimizing those mistakes is what eventually wins games, but it is important for your players to believe that if they play as best as they can, they won't be criticized because things didn't work out the way they liked.

Preparation

Finally, building confidence and overcoming fear of failure can be enhanced by taking the time to properly prepare. I have hard many of the great coaches talk about the will to prepare. To spend the necessary time on the practice field, in the weight room, and studying the playbooks and game plans to become successful. There is no shortcut to success and no substitute for hard work. We work toward consistent work habits on the field. Our coaches spend most of their time writing game plans, scouting reports, practice scripts, and written tests to help prepare our team mentally for each game. The more mentally prepared we can become from printed material and the more physically prepared we can become from practice will make everyone more confident about playing in the game. We want to eliminate the "what ifs" and replace them with "if whens." Cover as many situations as possible so the players won't panic when presented with something unexpected. Of course, all of this comes down to organization, and I had the privilege of working for 14 years under one the best organizers in the business, Coach Don James. I hope you'll find some of these ideas helpful. And as a close friend of mine tells his wife each time she leaves for the beauty shop… "Good luck to you!"

Dennis Parker is the head football coach at Mesa (AZ) High School, a position he assumed in 2005. A 1972 graduate of Southeast Oklahoma University, where he served as the captain of the Savage Storm football team as an offensive tackle, Parker has had an exceptional coaching career. In 1973, at the age of 24, he became the youngest head coach in the history of Texas 5A football when he took over the reins of the gridiron program at San Antonio Edison High School. Since then, he has compiled more than three decades of coaching experience in Texas, Missouri, and Arizona. His coaching achievements include winning two Texas state 5A championships (1983 with Converse Judson and 1990 with Marshall). For his efforts, he has twice been selected as the Texas high school football "Coach of the Year" (1988 and 1990).

Dennis' accomplishments extend well beyond the gridiron. In 1997, he became the first high school athletic director in the United States to implement mandatory drug testing of all athletes. He has served as a motivational speaker and trainer with the Zig Ziglar Corporation. He has hosted several television and radio shows. He has also written a weekly newspaper column. A gifted and much sought-after public speaker, he frequently works with businesses and college athletic teams on the process of goal setting. He continues to channel his interest in the benefits of and need for a values-oriented educational experience with his extensive efforts involving the development of character education curricula. In 2005, Dennis earned a Ph.D. in educational administration from Madison University.

Dennis and his wife, Mary, have two children, Kimberly—an elementary school teacher, and Sam—a high school football coach in Texas.

D.W. Rutledge is the executive director of the Texas High School Coaches Association—the largest association of its kind in the nation, a position he assumed in 2004. Rutledge is currently serving on the University Interscholastic League (UIL) Medical Advisory Committee of the Gatorade National Coaches Advisory Council and on the Board of Directors of the National Organization of Coaches Associations' Directors. Prior to his present position, D.W. was one of the most successful coaches in Texas high school football history. Rutledge served as an assistant coach from 1975-1983. In 17 seasons at Converse Judson, he compiled a 198-31-5 record, won 12 district championships, 10 city championships, 10 regional championships, and advanced the Rockets to the playoffs 16 times. In the process, his teams advanced to seven 5A state championship games, winning four in 1988, 1992, 1993, and 1995.

In 1985, D.W. was inducted in the Hall of Honor at Texas Lutheran College, where he captained the Bulldogs' 1974 national championship team and was a Kodak All-American linebacker for head coach Jim Wacker. In 1996, Texas Lutheran honored Rutledge with their "Distinguished Alumni Award". In the course of his illustrious coaching career, D.W. had received numerous honors for his coaching efforts, including being named "Coach of the Year" seven times. In addition, the *San Antonio Express News* named him football "Coach of the Decade" for the 80s and 90s. In 1996, he was selected to coach the South squad in the THSCA All-Star football game. In 1998, the *San Antonio Express News* accorded him "Greater San Antonio Sportsman of the Year" honors. In 2000, he was presented with the Tom Landry Award, recognizing him as "a positive role model and a credit to the coaching profession." In 2003, he was inducted into the "Texas High School Football Hall of Fame" in Waco, Texas, and in 2005, was inducted into the "Texas High School Coaches Association Hall of Honor."

D.W. and his wife, Kathy, have one son, Clint, who with his wife, Jamie, has blessed D.W. and Kathy with two grandchildren, Raylee and Ryder.

About the Authors